P9-BJB-834

261.52
F760

MYTHMAKERS,

GOSPEL, CULTURE, AND THE MEDIA

WILLIAM F. FORE

WITHDRAWN

LIBRARY ST. MARY'S COLLEGE

Friendship Press • New York

© 1990 by Friendship Press
Editorial Offices:
475 Riverside Drive, Room 772, New York, NY 10115
Distribution Offices:
P.O. Box 37844, Cincinnati, OH 45222-0844

All rights reserved. No part of this book may be reproduced in any
manner whatsoever without written permission of the publisher, except
brief quotations embodied in critical articles or reviews.

Manufactured in the United States of America
94 93 92 91 90   5 4 3 2 1

Library of Congress Cataloging-in-Publication Data

Fore, William F.
  Mythmakers : gospel, culture, and the media / William F. Fore.
    p.   cm.
  Includes bibliographical references.
  ISBN 0-377-00207-0
  1. Communication – Religious aspects – Christianity.   2. Mass media –
Religious aspects – Christianity.   3. Christianity and culture.
  4. Mass media – United States.   United States – Church
history – 20th century.   I. Title.
BV4319.F67   1990
  261.5′2–dc20   89-78167
                                                             CIP

To Emily, Matthias, Michael, and Mischa
— the next generation —
for the joy they bring
and the hope they represent

Contents

Introduction

Mythmakers and the Search for Meaning

> What good is it to me if Mary gave birth to the Son of God fourteen hundred years ago and I do not also give birth to the Son of God in my time and in my culture?
>
> –Meister Eckhart

The search for meaning is at the core of human life. It is not enough just to work and play and raise a family. We have a deep-seated need to be certain that our efforts are *worth it* — that our lives have meaning. One of theologian Paul Tillich's great contributions to religious understanding was to insist that what we mean by God is actually *that which is of ultimate meaning*. The search for meaning is the search for God.

This book is about that search, but from a special bias. It is the bias of the gospel — the good news that God liberates and frees people to be the children of God, that is, to be whole and filled with joy and satisfaction in their work, play, and families. It is a bias that affirms that for those to whom the Christian faith has meaning, the gospel brings peace and joy, and also the obligation to share it with others. For Christians, ultimate meaning — God — is understood in the person of Jesus Christ, in his life, death, and resurrection, and in the Holy Spirit, who allows us to see God present with us today.

But what do those words *mean* in today's secular society? Who was Jesus Christ in his life and death, and what do we mean by his resurrection? What do we mean by the Holy Spirit in this scientific age? How can we "see God" in a world filled with so many other claims? How can families "see God" when in the average American home the television set is on more than seven hours a day — every day? How can a high school senior "see God" when he reports: "I don't live in my house; I live in my room with my TV"?[1] How can young people "see God" when a teacher reports: "Many of the students thought that Shakespeare was born before Jesus; not one member of the same class knew who Cain and Abel were."[2]

The search for meaning inevitably forces us to look at our culture. The original meaning of culture comes from the Latin *colere*, to take care of, to preserve and cultivate. Culture is that which takes care of and preserves and cultivates our meanings and values. It is the system of beliefs and institutions that reflects the reality of our society. If we want to know who we are, who we can be, we have to look at our culture.

What Is Culture?

Imagine that culture is a large room filled with people. At the beginning of life, we enter the room. We see people talking and gesturing, laughing and crying, communicating in many ways. We listen. We learn their languages. We learn to read their facial expressions and their gestures. We exchange ideas. We express our feelings. We grow to understand their feelings and their emotions.

As we talk with more people, we learn a few new words and expressions, and we find that some words are used less and less, so we forget them. We continue to communicate — in order to be recognized, to be understood, to be somebody. Other people try to convince us of their ideas and views. We respond, and try to convince them of ours. Sometimes we even learn another language. The conversations go on, as we move slowly through the room. We influence a few here, reach out and help some others there. Things have changed, but only a little. To those who entered about the same time we did, we complain about some of the changes, mourn some of the losses. Finally we grow tired of the interchange, and so we slip out through a door at the far end of the room, our exit scarcely noticed. The room is still full of people. The conversations continue.

Culture both reflects and shapes our values and our worldview. And during the last one hundred and fifty years, since the invention of the telegraph in 1844, a sea change has swept across our North American culture, changing the way it is expressed, and thus changing the culture itself. The culture has come to be expressed primarily through the mass media of communication, and one medium more than any other: television. Television has become the great cultivator of our culture.

What Are Myths?

The most powerful tools of culture, and especially its mass media expressions, are its *myths*. By myths we do not mean untruths or "belivin' what you know ain't so." Just the contrary: in this book, by myths we mean *stories that unfold or explain the worldview of a people*. In the ancient world, the most powerful people were the mythmakers. It is the same today, and today our most powerful mythmakers are the mass media.

Christians, on the other hand, have always marched to a different drummer. Their Scriptures also express myths, stories that unfold and explain the Christian worldview. Their myths are different from the media myths. In his essay "Religion and Literature," T. S. Eliot neatly summed up the challenge this brings: "So long as we are conscious of the gulf fixed between ourselves [as Christians] and the greater part of contemporary [culture], we are more or less protected from being harmed by it, and are in a position to extract from it what good it has to offer us."[3]

Thus our search for meaning requires us to look at our Christian gospel on one hand and our mass-mediated culture on the other, and then try to bring them together in ways that neither violate the spirit of the gospel nor ignore the reality of the culture. The search requires us to examine the gospel, the culture and the media — the *mythmakers* of our time.

The task of this book is *to suggest how Christians can relate their understanding of the gospel to their culture, especially as communicated by the mass media*. We will look at the mythmakers, and sort out which myths *we* wish to use in cultivating our culture, so that, when it is our time to slip out a door at the end of the room, we will leave behind a culture where the really important things of life are discussed and celebrated.

In writing this book, I bring several assumptions:

1. That if theological thinking is to be meaningful today, it must be grounded in ordinary experience.

2. That Christians are always part of a Christian tradition, and that tradition is indebted to the Scriptures.

3. That the Scriptures are always interpreted and understood within the cultures of Christians of different times and places.

4. That the language of Christian tradition has lost much of its meaning and no longer speaks clearly and authoritatively to people in our culture or, indeed, to many people in the churches of North America.

5. That the task of Christians today — as in every age — is to allow the gospel to speak with new relevance by using stories and images which grow out of our own experience.

6. That the mass media in general, and TV in particular, always communicate messages, and that these messages are especially important because they are seen to be trivial and unimportant.

7. That television and other mass media are not inherently evil, but that because of the way they are used, the messages they carry are contending with institutional religion for dominance in articulating our values, assumptions, and worldview.

8. That the problems of life are not necessarily out of control, and that situations can be changed.

9. That when things are not as they should be, our task is to identify the underlying causes of the problems and then work to expose and change what is wrong.

These are my assumptions, and I hope that the reading this book will convince you to make some of them yours.

1

What Does "the Gospel" Really Mean?

> And he told them many things in parables....
> —Matthew 13:3
> And he taught them many things in parables....
> —Mark 4:2
> He told them a parable also....
> —Luke 5:36
> I have said this to you in parables....
> —John 16:25

The phone rang in my office. Dan Potter, executive director of the New York City Council of Churches, was calling to say he was in trouble. It was the early spring of 1963, and since I had been in the new Methodist Board of Missions offices at the Interchurch Center only a few months, I still enjoyed swivelling my desk chair around to look out my picture window. On a clear day, I could see the Ramapo Mountains some twenty miles away beyond the Hudson River.

"We have a problem," Dan said. "There are just a few months left until the New York World's Fair begins, and we can't get going on our film for the Protestant Pavilion. Can you help?"

A few days later three "film doctors" — Lois Anderson from the American Baptist Churches, John Bachman from Union Theological Seminary, and I — were ushered into a room filled with representatives of Protestant New York, forty-three people from organizations across the religious spectrum, including every group

5

from rock-bound fundamentalists to far-out liberals. We were supposed to create order out of chaos.

For two years they had been meeting, and disagreeing, regularly. Script after script had been rejected, proposals scuttled, formats abandoned. Today, as usual, they glowered at one another across the table. Then the representative from the Salvation Army made a suggestion that posed both the solution and the problem.

"Why don't we produce a film that just tells the simple gospel story?" he said. There were vigorous nods; everyone agreed. That's what we need! The BASIC GOSPEL STORY! Then, for two hours, everyone disagreed over what the basic gospel story *was*. For some, it was John 3:16. For others, it was the Sermon on the Mount. Conservatives wanted Luke, literally, while liberals wanted John, metaphorically. Some wanted the miracles in, others wanted them out. And, of course, what *version* of the Bible would be used? Would Jesus talk in Old English or up-to-date American? And so on.

We left that meeting in a daze. Something had to be done, and fairly quickly. The World's Fair was fast approaching, and the Protestant Council of New York was building a beautiful new movie theater on the fair grounds just for the film — *our* film — which was supposed to rival Michelangelo's *Pietà*, being shipped over from Rome by the Catholics.

We went to Rolf Forsberg, one of the most creative filmmakers we knew. We asked him to talk with Harvey Cox, a theologian with experience in television and film. They talked for two days. Rolf knew an old circus town in Wisconsin that had fascinating visuals. Harvey knew all about historic Christ symbols, including the clown.

And so they proposed to us, and we proposed to the committee, a film with no dialogue, no scenes of the Holy Land, no Bible characters. Instead, the film would be about a clown who comes riding into town on a donkey. He's part of a rather motley circus; he experiences the human failings of the circus people; he encounters the magician Magnus, who wants to dominate and control; he substitutes himself for a poor human-puppet and is killed by Magnus. But then Magnus himself puts on the clown's white face, and at the end, the clown rides again into the next town — with the circus of life.

And they loved it! In half an hour they agreed to it after not agreeing on anything else in two years. They agreed because every man and woman on that committee saw in it his or her *own* understanding of "the basic gospel story." They knew what the gospel meant to *them*, and they saw the gospel in this story.

What we had proposed was a parable. The film was produced, and *Parable* became a hit of the New York World's Fair; thirty years later it still enjoys vigorous circulation as a discussion starter among youth and adults who want to explore the meaning of Jesus and the gospel story.

I learned two important lessons from that experience. One is that it is truly impossible for any of us to uncover the "real" gospel story, because the "real" gospel story always comes to us wrapped in a cultural history we can never fully understand. In fact, the more scholars penetrate into the biblical record, the more enigmatic and uncertain that record becomes. Let's explore this further before going on to the second lesson I learned that day.

Did Jesus Say That?

In 1985 a group of thirty Protestant and Roman Catholic scholars from colleges and seminaries across the United States began to meet to consider the written statements of Jesus in the light of the idioms, history, and cultural setting of his time, and so to try to determine which statements are "authentic" and which are not. Called the Jesus Seminar, the group meets twice each year, and thus far they have agreed that Jesus did not say many of the things attributed to him.

For example, they think that only three of a dozen "blessings" and "woes" from the Gospels of Matthew and Luke actually come from Jesus. Those considered authentic include, from Luke: "Blessed are you poor...you that hunger...you that weep." But "Blessed are the peacemakers, for they shall be called the children of God," and "the meek...shall inherit the earth" are both unlikely to have been said by Jesus. Rather, these sayings come from traditions well known before the time of Jesus.[1]

Also, say these scholars, the Lord's Prayer probably was not composed by Jesus at all, but more likely was composed by early Christians after the crucifixion. Only four lines ("hallowed be thy name/thy kingdom come/give us this day our daily bread/and forgive us our debts") may paraphrase things Jesus actually said during his lifetime, though the seminar members think it unlikely Jesus ever put these lines together in a single prayer.

Robert W. Funk, New Testament scholar and organizer of the

Jesus Seminar, points out that all four New Testament Gospels were written forty years or more after Jesus' crucifixion, and although church tradition says that the disciples Matthew and John both wrote Gospels, Bible scholars for more than a century have believed that none of the Gospel writers actually knew Jesus during his lifetime. Instead, these authors were dependent on written and oral accounts that had already undergone interpretation and were based on traditions built up to reflect needs and expectations of early believers. For example, many biblical scholars long ago concluded that both Matthew and Luke drew much of their writings from Mark, and that much of their additional material came from a document called "Q." This explains why there are many similar sayings in Matthew and Luke: the writers we know as "Matthew" and "Luke" incorporated material from both Mark and "Q" into their testaments. The Jesus Seminar group believes that the Lord's Prayer also probably originated with "Q."[2]

What Is "the Gospel"?

Over the centuries, biblical scholars have offered widely differing views about "the gospel." In the fourth century, St. Jerome, one of the first true scholars of the church and translator of the Old and New Testaments into what became the *Vulgate** Bible, asserted that everything written in the Bible is literally true. For the next thousand years the Bible was generally seen as divinely inspired and unassailably accurate in every detail.

However, the Reformation of the church that became widespread in the sixteenth century depended heavily on translations of the Bible into languages spoken in the various European countries of the time. Martin Luther, for example, not only translated the Bible into German, but interpreted the Gospels in printed sermons as well. When such other Reformers as John Calvin and, later, Roger Williams disagreed *in print* with Luther on, for example, what the Scriptures said about the role of government in society, the whole matter of biblical interpretation was opened to thousands of individuals who for the first time could read (or have read to them) the published documents.

---

*So-called because Jerome translated the Bible from the unfamiliar Greek and Semitic languages into the Latin commonly spoken at the time ("vulgar" comes from the Latin for "mob" or "common people"). Jerome's "revised version" thus became the most widely used Bible in the Western church.

By the eighteenth century, scholars began to subject the Scriptures to the same kind of scientific inquiry they were applying to their observations of the natural world. Faith alone no longer provided sufficient explanation. The late eighteenth-century Age of Reason pressed this approach even further, seeking to discover the historical reality behind the Scriptures. One of these early "scientific" scholars of the Bible was Thomas Jefferson who, shortly after he left the White House in 1809, wrote a biography of Jesus, "abstracting what is really his [Jesus'] from the rubbish in which it is buried, easily distinguished by its luster from the dross of his biographers, and as separable from that as the diamond from the dung hill."[3]

By the nineteenth and early twentieth centuries, biblical scholars, mainly in Germany, were sifting out the "dross" of the Gospels in an attempt to get behind the words to the flesh and blood Jesus. The most famous of their researches was Albert Schweitzer's biography, *The Quest for the Historical Jesus.* By 1926 New Testament theologian Rudolf Bultmann concluded that all such attempts to find the "real" Jesus were fruitless, because the Bible is so full of legends and unprovable events that "we can now know almost nothing concerning the life and personality of Jesus."[4]

But still the search goes on for the meanings, if not the facts, in the Hebrew and Greek Scriptures. More ancient documents continued to be discovered. Today, some biblical scholars, such as Phyllis Trible, concentrate on writing styles, convinced that biblical authors had revealing ways of constructing their narratives. Others, like Thomas Oden, have discovered that Jewish culture provides important understandings about Jesus and the gospel. For example, says Oden, "There is evidence that Jesus taught his disciples to recall his teachings by heart. We have the *ipsissima verba*, the exact words of Jesus. Why should they have been reported if they hadn't been actually remembered?"[5] And theologian Edward Schillebeeckx writes, "In the historical man Jesus there must be present some ground or reason for our being able to acknowledge him [as Christ]."[6]

Clearly, people who became Christians were responding to *something.* Jesus was a superb communicator. He took into account the cultural setting of his audience. As theologian Lucien Richard says, "He had to speak a language they could understand, perform actions they would find intelligible, and conduct his life and undergo his death in a manner of which they could make some sense."[7]

But exactly what he said and exactly how he acted comes to us filtered, for all time, through those who saw and heard him: "The only knowledge we possess of the Christ event reaches us via the concrete experience of the first local communities of Christians who were sensitive of a new life present in them."[8] Reports of that experience were fragmentary and always filtered through the needs and expectations of the men and women in that first believing community.

And what were those needs and expectations?

> The first community, in order to affirm that Jesus was more than one of the prophets — that his authority had a certain finality or absoluteness about it not found in others — had few options left to it but to tell the story of Jesus in such a way that his authority would become apparent and would confront other hearers, as it had confronted those who had witnessed it, with the necessity to make up their minds — to declare themselves for or against Jesus.[9]

Telling the Truth as Story

When we want to speak the truth about something we have learned that has transformed our life, we often are inspired to tell it as a story. The men and women of the first century who experienced the Christ event in their own lives found themselves in exactly this situation:

> Honest [people] try to tell the truth, but in order to do so they are obliged, like liars, to tell stories.... Stories have been told, and told with imagination, in the serious attempt to speak the truth that concerns human life most deeply.[10]

Telling the truth as story explains why the New Testament continues to be such an imaginative and compelling work, and also why it cannot be taken "literally." Amos Wilder, the scholar of literature and religion, has written that "the New Testament writings are in large part works of the imagination, loaded, charged and encrusted with every kind of figurative resource and invention."[11] Another biblical scholar, Sallie McFague, confronts biblical literalism head on: "This may be blasphemy to the literal-minded; but it is fortunate that the New Testament writers were endowed with rich imaginations, for otherwise the New Testament would hold little chance of being revelatory."[12]

But even when we understand why, for example, the New Testament writers went to great pains to confirm Jesus' birth in Old Testament predictions of a Savior, or to relate his genealogical lineage to King David, or to tie his betrayal and death to other Old Testament prophecies ("so that the Scriptures might be fulfilled") — we still are left with a fragmentary puzzle instead of a clear picture of the "real" Jesus. For example, if we had only the writings of Paul (which probably were the very earliest reports about Jesus to have been written down), we would never have read that Jesus ever taught in parables or proverbs, since all of that information was written in the four Gospels *after* Paul wrote his letters to the young churches.

In sum, while we probably have as much information about Jesus as any other historical figure of his time, the information is sketchy and, above all, filtered through the minds and the culture of the early Christian community. As Yale historian Jaroslav Pelikan says: "...the presentation of Jesus in the New Testament is in fact itself a representation: it resembles a set of paintings more closely than it does a photograph."[13]

Many Christians recognize that their knowledge of the findings of history as well as of the natural and human sciences today makes it no longer possible for them to treat claims made in the Scriptures in the same ways that Christians did centuries ago. David Tracy, a theologian who analyzes the clash between faith and science, says, "To continue to uphold a literal interpretation of the Genesis account is simply and irrevocably impossible for anyone who accepts the findings of the modern physical and life sciences. To continue to believe a literalist theory of scriptural inspiration seems no longer an option to anyone who has investigated the results of modern historical study of the scriptures."[14]

But Tracy does not conclude therefore that the Christian faith must crumble before the onslaught of science, and neither should we. He points out that the task of theologians must be to remain true to the church-community of which they are members, while at the same time being committed to the methods and insights of current scholarly inquiry. Indeed, this is the task of every Christian, and it is important to stress that the two approaches are not incompatible. *Christians can be both true to the faith, and at the same time true to the canons of modern scientific inquiry.* Indeed, many Christians believe that the same spirit of truth works through both knowledge and faith.

The Gospel as Parable

Our understanding of the meaning of the gospel is helped considerably by the fact that the Scriptures are clothed in parables and metaphors. Parables are familiar stories that embody unfamiliar and significant truths. Metaphors are words that do the same thing: they help us see the ordinary world in extraordinary ways. If parables and metaphors are taken literally, they lose their meaning. A parable can speak about God being like a father who welcomes his wayward son home. It may describe the Kingdom of God as being like a mustard seed, tiny but with great potential, or like the leaven a woman kneads into the dough to transform the whole loaf, or like a wedding feast to which all are invited. The Gospels speak in very human terms, but in terms that draw connections in our minds — *that* event with *our* events, *that* time with *our* times, *that* relationship with *our* relationships.

The Gospels do not drift into mystical abstractions or propose complicated theological systems. In fact, they are very anthropomorphic, that is, they describe ultimate reality in very human terms: parent, child, weeping, rejoicing. But, as Elizabeth Sewell says, what else *could* they do? "Human beings cannot think or move in nonhuman ways: given what we are, we must think and move 'anthropomorphically.' "[15]

In her helpful book *Speaking in Parables*, Sallie McFague has written that the most significant parts of the New Testament consist of parables: "...as New Testament scholars agree, the parables not only are Jesus' most characteristic form of teaching but are among the most authentic strata in the New Testament."[16] In fact, she holds, the entire New Testament is itself a kind of parable. She points out that even the letters of Paul are "on a continuum with the parable." That is, Paul's letters are close to oral speech, using dialogue, accusation, defense, and exclamations that grab the reader. They also contain a great deal of confession, so that Paul "not only uses himself, but he thinks in and through himself: he takes himself as a human metaphor."[17]

McFague argues that the parable is the preeminent form of Christian witness and proclamation, because it can express the deeper dimensions of human existence in lively, compelling ways. In this regard, the parable is a key to how we need to communicate "the gospel" story *today*, for parables provides a necessary corrective to the increasingly word-bound, stultifying, and just plain boring Protestant theology that has developed during the last two centuries — "a battle over words and what they mean." To the extent that our religion has become reduced to words, and even to words used to explain words — in the worship service, in the Scriptures, in life itself — it ceases to have life-giving properties. But through parables and their retelling we find a clue to how "the gospel" can be communicated in every age, including our own.

Meanings Are in People

This brings me to the second important lesson learned from my experience with the film *Parable*. I learned that meanings are in people, that is, meanings, including the meanings of "the gospel," are not "out there" somewhere as an object, like a star or a microbe. Rather, *there are no meanings except as people give meanings to things and relationships*. The reason that meanings are not "out there," independent of people, is simply because meanings arise from human relationships themselves; in fact, they exist *in* the relationships. If you don't believe it, try to imagine a meaning that is *not* connected in some way to a person.

Of course the world abounds in verifiable data that we can confirm. There are rules of geometry and mathematical tables that do not change (though we may stop using them). Trees fall in the forest, whether or not we are there to hear them. Things do exist "out there." But the *meanings* of things depend upon people and their relationship to other people and things. The same event may mean one thing to me, and something quite different to you, and both of us may (or may not) be "right." To my mother I am a son; to my wife I am a husband; to my daughter I am a father — and they are all right. Why is the location of meaning so important? Because when we deal with religion, we deal with seismic emotions. People feel deeply about their faith, about its veracity, its verifiability, its reality, its meaning to them. Yet we get no farther than that committee of forty-three did with their World's Fair film if we insist that *our* gospel is *the* gospel, that the meaning the gospel has for me is somehow the Truth (with a capital T), while the meaning all others derive from it is only partial Truth or, in some cases, actual Falsehood. Such thinking has launched endless bloody inquisitions throughout history, most of them justified on the basis that it is better to mutilate the flesh than to allow Falsehood to destroy the soul.

The Last Temptation of Christ

A good example of the clash over meanings is the 1988 controversy about *The Last Temptation of Christ*, a film version of the novel by Nikos Kazantzakis. As the studio heads and theater owners were picketed and attackers and supporters tossed their quotable quotes at each other and the press, magazines, newspapers, and TV stations gleefully recorded the events.

The diversity of opinions was exceeded only by their intensity. Jerry Falwell said that Hollywood "...has never stooped so low. *The Last Temptation of Christ* is utter blasphemy of the worst degree. Neither the label 'fiction' nor the First Amendment gives Universal the right to libel, slander and ridicule the most central figure in world history...." Donald Wildmon charged: "The script...is the most perverted, distorted account of the historical and biblical Jesus I have ever read."[18] Bill Bright, of Campus Crusade for Christ, said, "Universal Pictures will always be remembered as the studio that launched an attack on the sanctity of all religions by making a film which blasphemes and demeans our Lord Jesus Christ. This time the Christians are not going to forget."[19]

On the other hand, Paul Moore, Episcopal bishop of New York, affirmed: "The movie is artistically excellent and theologically sound....Christ is presented as a muscular, strong, manly person who sweated, bled, had doubts and was, as the Bible says, 'tempted in every way yet without sin.'"[20] Joseph Brownrigg, a United Methodist with a Ph.D. in film and theology, called the film "the best Jesus movie that has ever been made."[21] And Andrew Greeley, priest and author, wrote: "...the film makes us think about who God is — that is to say, what life means. If I were a pastor I'd take advantage of that challenge. I'd urge my adult education group to see *The Last Temptation* and then compare its imagery with that to be found in the four gospels and especially in the parables. Out of such a comparison would come, I think, a fruitful re-evaluation of who Jesus was and what He was."[22]

Let us put aside questions about the film's merits in favor of a much more important issue: what was really going on here? The answer is: a clash over the *meaning* of "meaning," in this case, the meaning of Jesus and the gospel to individuals. Some believed that their Truth was objective, one-hundred-percent accurate and permanent, and that for anyone to understand or portray it otherwise (as through this film) would be harmful to the Truth, to those who "have" the Truth, and even harmful to the portrayers. Others believed their truth was subjective and personal, something they developed over time, something neither final nor totally accurate, though they believed it was based on the best available evidence.

This kind of conflict is not going to go away. It will keep reappearing in different guises. So long as there are highly motivated people who believe their Truth is the only Truth, while others believe that such an absolute position is unsupportable and harmful, we will continue to have inquisitions, Holy Wars, and film boycotts — and the gospel will continue to be misunderstood and misused.

I believe that what is important about Jesus and the gospel is the experience that the people who followed Jesus had, the *meaning* they found in his life and death and resurrection, and consequently the meaning it can have for people today. We can never directly experience what first-century Christians experienced, but we must try to understand their experience using our best tools of analysis. And we must similarly try to understand the "cloud of witnesses," those Christians of every earlier generation, who had their own unique understandings, interpretations, and testimonies. We must seek to know what *they* meant by the gospel. Then, equipped with the best possible understanding of what the faith has meant to Christians over the centuries, we must develop our *own* meaning — and seek to communicate it to others in ways they can understand in today's culture.

That is the agenda of this book — to relate earlier meanings of the gospel with today's culture, especially our media culture, so we may know, interpret, be transformed, and speak from our experience today.

Our next step is to look more closely at the way Christian believers in the past, that "cloud of witnesses," have found meaning in Jesus and the gospel throughout the Christian Era, and how their cultures influenced their own search for meaning. In so doing, we will shed more light on our own situation as their heirs.

2

How Christians Interpret the Gospel

> We live not by things,
> but by the meaning of things.
> It is needful to transmit the passwords
> from generation to generation.
> —Antoine de Saint-Exupery

The Gospels in the New Testament are only the beginning of "the gospel." "The gospel" has a second source which is not found in the written record of the Bible at all: the historical witness and testimony of almost twenty centuries of Christian believers. While Jesus' life, death, and resurrection are essential elements in the Christian experience, so are the faith responses of Christians throughout history, and both are part of the gospel in our time.

For almost two thousand years Christians have been interpreting the gospel in terms of what they knew about the Old and New Testaments, their own cultures, their media, and their experiences. Each generation of believers has incorporated its own life and times into what the gospel means. So we need to know something about that interpretation over the centuries, because it forms a crucial living link between Jesus and ourselves.

The Gospel Always Comes Wrapped in a Cultural Context

As we said in Chapter 1, we simply can never expect to transport ourselves back to first-century Palestine and experience the "real" gospel in its "real" culture. That very human desire was the trap that the "quest for the historical Jesus" scholars fell into. ality, there is no "real" gospel except as it has been trans to us in the Bible and through the faithful for whom it h~~ ~ad meaning over the centuries. Each generation has had to face anew the question "Who is Jesus?" and to work out its own answers, in terms of its own culture.

The gospel *always* comes wrapped in a particular language, particular customs and traditions and ways of doing things, particular unwritten rules about politics and religion and the family — in other words, in a particular culture. Culture has many complicated meanings, but I use it here simply to describe a system of beliefs (about God or reality or ultimate meaning), of values (about what is true, good, and beautiful), of customs (about how to behave and relate to others), and of the institutions which express the culture (government, church, law courts, family, school, and so on) — all of which bind the society together and give it meaning.[1]

We can never get completely "out" of our culture. Our culture was there before we were born into it, and we became human as we interacted with it. While we may pick and choose to emphasize certain aspects of it, and even change it slightly during our lifetime, our culture is like the air we breathe — something we take for granted, but without which we would cease to be who and what we are.

In the last two thousand years, Christianity has been experienced in many different cultures. Therefore, Christians have interpreted Christianity in widely different ways over the centuries. Jaroslav Pelikan, an eminent church historian, has devoted an entire book to the ways people of different times have understood Jesus. He shows that "for each age, the life and teachings of Jesus represented an answer (or, more often *the* answer) to the most fundamental questions of human existence and of human destiny, and it was to the figure of Jesus as set forth in the gospels that those questions were addressed."[2]

The Jesus of History

During the first three hundred or so years after Jesus, Christians regarded their gatherings not as a society for the promotion of personal salvation but as a way of proclaiming the Lordship of the God of Jesus, the God of love, peace, and justice. According to Lesslie Newbigin, the message of Jesus to these early followers "was about the kingship, the universal sovereignty of God. It was not a message about the interior life of the soul considered in abstraction from the public life of the world."[3]

Newbigin places these first-century Christians and their role in society in stark contrast to the role of churches in the Western world today. If these early followers had been content to withdraw from and forget their relationship to the rest of society, Newbigin says, they would have posed no threat to the Emperor and his power: the first-century church "would have enjoyed the protection of the law — the same protection which churches enjoy in our modern culture, available for exactly the same reason — namely, that they pose no threat to the ideology which controls public life."[4] Instead, Christians refused to bow the knee to Rome, because Almighty God, not the Emperor, was the Lord of all. They called their gathering the *ecclesia Theou*, the assembly of God — a public assembly to which all humankind were summoned and which was called together not by the town clerk but by God, an assembly where no earthly emperor could claim absolute supremacy. This was the kind of assembly Roman power could not permit. Therefore, Christians understood their lot to include persecution and, often, torture and death, and they lived in hope of the return of Jesus: "Truly, I say unto you, this generation will not pass away till all these things take place. Heaven and earth will pass away, but my words will not pass away" (Matt. 24:34; Mark 13:30; Luke 21:32). Evidence of their persecuted status is still visible in Rome, where the catacombs reveal thousands of martyrs' bones, and rude stone caskets record hundreds of deaths in the faith.

By the fourth century a shift in the status of Christianity affected the understanding of the gospel. A Roman Emperor, Constantine, passed from paganism to Christianity. History is ambiguous about the reasons for his conversion, but we do know that in 312, at the Battle of the Milvian Bridge, "Constantine was directed in a dream to cause a heavenly sign to be delineated on the shields of his soldiers, and so to proceed to battle."[5] He marked his shields with the Chi-Rho (in Greek, the first two letters of "Christ"), an emblem of Christianity. The battle was won, and shortly thereafter Constantine declared Christianity the official religion of the Empire. When he built Constantinople as the New Rome, he constructed the huge Hagia Sophia, one of the grandest of all churches. In its southern gallery one can still see today a golden mosaic depicting the Constantinian transformation to imperial (and triumphal) Christianity: Christ as King (*Pantocrator*) is seated in the center on a throne, flanked by the Emperor Constantine on one side and the Empress Zoe on the other. Spiritual and temporal power were united.

This understanding of the gospel as earthly power resulted in struggles for authority and territory between medieval European rulers and the Western church centered in Rome. This perspective also set in motion the Crusades that flourished from the eleventh to the fourteenth centuries. To "take up the Cross" meant literally to sew a red cross on one's garment and to go off to war against the Turks in Palestine. As judged by a modern historian, Steven Runciman, this "crusading fervor always provided an excuse for killing God's enemies" — in Jesus' name.[6]

But another understanding of Jesus and the gospel began to take form in the early centuries of the church. During the Middle Ages this view became increasingly institutionalized in the monastic movement. Thousands of men and women who turned to a cloistered life patterned themselves closely after Christ. And "by the time they were finished," Pelikan observes, they "were likewise patterning Christ after themselves." Through the monastic life they demonstrated how to "share by patience in the passion of Christ and hereafter deserve to be united with him in his kingdom." Theirs was a simple, direct formula: "not to value anything more highly than the love of Christ."[7]

St. Francis of Assisi is perhaps the most revered of those who understood Jesus in terms of his humility, poverty, and self denial. Early in the thirteenth century, Francis created a monastic order founded on the principle of conformity to the life of Jesus "in all things." Toward the end of his life this principle was dramatized when "the marks of nails began to appear in his hands and feet, just as he had seen them in the vision of the Man nailed to the Cross."[8] For thousands of followers of Francis, Jesus became the literal model for all of life. Those in religious orders did not all withdraw from the world. Many monks and nuns, in response to the gospel stories of Jesus' ministry, became active in the world, serving as missionaries to areas of Europe not yet Christian, caring for the poor, preaching and teaching.

In the Middle Ages the church was the institution that preserved documents and provided most education. But the gospel story itself was communicated to most of the faithful through pictures, carvings, stained glass, drama, music, and spoken words rather than through books. During the fourteenth and fifteenth centuries, the understanding of Jesus and the gospel emerged in a renewed way into daily life. Gospel stories were often consciously allegorized into everyday terms. Painting, especially in Italy, became a valued means of communication, through such artists as Giotto, Botticelli, and Leonardo da Vinci. The Bible came to life on their canvasses, as every parable, saying, and deed of Jesus' life was rendered in vivid color and with increasing realism and depth of perspective. The culture of the time guided the artist's eye. The Madonna became a round and rosy Italian maid, the Baby Jesus a bouncing Italian bambino, while Roman governors, disciples, saints, and martyrs were all depicted as medieval Italians against an Italian landscape.

To the north in sixteenth-century Flanders and Germany, the genius of Peter Brueghel and Albrecht Dürer brought the Bible to life for anyone who could see their paintings and drawings. Old and New Testament figures became *burghers* and *hausfraulein*, and the biblical scenes were set among the familiar barns, haylofts, farmhouses, and countryside of everyday life.

The understanding of the gospel in the culture of its time reaches a musical apex in the eighteenth century. In the *St. Matthew Passion* and *St. John Passion*, as well as many of his cantatas, Johann Sebastian Bach portrayed the gospel story in vivid, dramatic detail. The Evangelist tells the story in direct narrative style, soloists act out the various roles of Jesus, Mary, the High Priest, Peter, and others, while the chorus comments on the betrayal, death, and resurrection. The story was old, the musical setting the work of genius, but the music, at the time, was *familiar;* Bach employed scores of earlier hymns and even popular songs, and of course the language was German, with the result that the average Protestant churchgoing listener had a new experience — the words and music of the time were recast to provide religious relevance and meaning.

Of all the interpretations of the gospel during the nineteenth and twentieth centuries, few were more direct and at the same time more communicative than hymns. A century earlier John Wesley and his brother Charles had written hundreds of hymns that stirred working-class people in England, and this tradition continued in America through such writers as Timothy Dwight, Samuel Longfellow, Oliver Wendell Holmes, and more recently

Henry Sloane Coffin and Harry Emerson Fosdick. While hymns covered just about every subject, those that found particular favor in nineteenth-century America were based on a personal experience of Jesus and the gospel, particularly in regard to faith ("Blessed Assurance, Jesus Is Mine"), the atonement of Jesus ("When I Survey the Wondrous Cross"), confession ("Just As I Am, Without One Plea"), dedication ("Nearer, My God, to Thee"), following Jesus' example ("Saviour, Like a Shepherd Lead Us"), and salvation ("Amazing Grace! How Sweet the Sound").

Our own century provides understandings of Jesus and the gospel that in some ways differ from previous understandings but nonetheless are linked to earlier traditions. Think of the coronations in the United Kingdom, where the civil head of state is crowned in Westminster Abbey by the Archbishop of Canterbury attended by all the prelates of the church, in a centuries-old religious ceremony replete with choirs, trumpet fanfares and processionals, seen and heard worldwide by millions on radio and television. Similar coverage is accorded the pope's visits to North America and other continents, including special jets, cars with special bullet-proof glass, hordes of police and press — a modern-day evocation of the church triumphant that goes back more than a thousand years.

In stark contrast, this century also witnessed Gandhi's Long March to the sea, which, because it was picked up by London and New York newspapers, focused world attention on the plight of the Indians under their British rulers. Later the world saw a similar drama, this time on television, enacted in Selma and Birmingham, as Martin Luther King, Jr., joined hands with religious leaders from throughout the United States to protest against injustices, which led to major legal reform in civil rights. In both cases, the image of the gospel displayed to participants and spectators alike was Jesus' emphasis on community, suffering for others, and self-giving love.

Other twentieth-century views of Jesus have aroused widespread response. Picasso's *Guernica* depicted the horrors of the bombing by Nazi planes of a tiny village during the Spanish Civil War, making striking use of the cross to drive home the inhumanity of modern warfare. In a score of powerful *Miserere* paintings and prints, Georges Rouault interpreted suffering and death as the essence of Jesus' way. Fellini's film *Jesus of Nazareth* emphasized the starkness of Jesus' time; its image of the Sermon on the Mount delivered in a howling storm is unforgettable. A few years ago in Canada, empathy and protest were aroused by Almuth Lutkenhaus's sculpture *Christa*, in which the figure on the cross was female.

These scattered examples illustrate that Christians of every generation have needed to come to terms with the meaning of the gospel of Jesus, and that they have expressed their understanding *in terms of their own life and times*. We cannot judge whether any particular understanding was more or less "true" than that of another generation, but we must understand that, for those Christians, *it was true*. It was by that particular understanding of the gospel, wrapped in the culture of their days, that people guided their lives, spent their time, took certain actions and avoided others. In a sense, they "bet their lives" on the meanings of the gospel they found, created, and celebrated within their own culture. Our challenge today is to engage in a similar process of understanding, creation, and commitment.

The Jesus of Geography

The meaning of the gospel depends not merely on time but also on location. Today the gospel is given very different interpretations by people in different cultural settings.

A few years ago in Japan, my wife and I visited an old friend, Masao Takenaka, professor of Christian ethics at Doshisha University in Kyoto, the spiritual center of Japan. One afternoon Masao led us to a lovely garden behind his office where we were served tea according to the traditional ceremony, sitting on straw tatami mats and using hand-molded cups three centuries old. Then he presented us with his book called *Christian Art in Asia*, the very first compilation of the works of Asian artists on Christian themes. In those pages the gospel is made flesh within the Asian experience: Jesus calling Japanese fishermen; the nativity in a Korean barn; a beautiful Indian *Blue Madonna*; an Indonesian Madonna and child; an Indian Last Supper; a Sri Lankan Christ; a crucifixion in the midst of the Philippines.

Two decades earlier I experienced other unique gospel interpretations, this time in Africa, most often through music. I shall never forget visiting a Methodist girls' school in what is now Zimbabwe, where, for a foreign visitor, the teenagers sang "Just As I Am, Without One Plea" to an accompaniment of rattles, drums, tinkling spoons, and Coke bottles, and at a pace and syncopation that simply made you want to dance.

And in Bolivia, where I had gone to make a film about missionary activity, the music again was Christian, and again unique. This time a young woman, completely uneducated, came into a studio in La Paz, ten thousand feet high in the Andes, and sang lullabies and folk songs that sounded as if she had been studying music all her life. The record sold thousands of copies, long before the Beatles and others discovered the riches of Bolivian folk music. But this folk music was transformed by a Christian perspective.

Of course, wherever one encounters Latin American Christianity, there is music, whether in the streets of Rio de Janeiro or Caracas or Miami or Los Angeles. Singing and dancing are a way of life, and Christian interpretations of Jesus' life, death, and resurrection are commemorated in dozens of Latin American festivals and carnivals. In 1988, when Latin American and North American Christian communicators met in San Juan, Puerto Rico, a highlight of the week was the presentation of indigenous songs and dance by Puerto Rican Christians who carry on a rich and sophisticated religious musical tradition for the sheer joy of it.

One of the most powerful cultural interpretations of the gospel came to America through the experience of African slaves. James Weldon Johnson celebrated the unique sermon style of black preaching in his book *God's Trombones*, which includes a famous passage from "The Creation":

> Then down between
> The darkness and the light
> He hurled the world;
> And God said: That's good![9]

Martin Luther King, Jr., was formed in this tradition, and he used it to create a preaching style that stirred the moral imagination of both black and white audiences and was a significant element in validating his leadership of the civil rights movement. For example, imagine King's voice as he told his congregation at Ebenezer Baptist Church in Atlanta how it will be when *God* judges the world:

Oh, there will be a day. The question won't be how many awards did you get in life. Not that day. It won't be how popular were you in your social setting. That won't be the question that day.... The question that day will not be concerned whether you are a Ph.D. or a No.D, will not be concerned whether you went to Morehouse or... No House.... On that day the question will be what did you do for others. Now I can hear somebody saying, "Lord, uh, I did a lot of things in Life. I did my job well.... I went to school and studied hard. I accumulated a lot of money, Lord, that's what I did." Seems as if I can hear the Lord of Light saying, "But I was hungry, and you fed me not. I was sick and ye visited me not. I was *neck*-id in the cold, and I was in prison and you weren't concerned about me, so get out of my face!"[10]

The spirituals, the participatory sermon styles ("Amen!"... "God Almighty!"), the dynamic worship experiences — all testify that African-Americans found ways to express their gospel of liberation, freedom, and salvation in the midst of oppression and hardship in America. A contribution not yet so well recognized is that of the Native Americans, bringing profound identification with nature, deep appreciation of the continuity of all things, and a connectedness with ancestors that has greatly enriched religion in North America.

Finally, popular music, while not great poetry, is nevertheless full of metaphor and meaning, and some of it sees the gospel in the light of secular experience. An example is "The Tree Springs to Life," from a contemporary hymnal:

> They hung him in Jerusalem,
> And in Hiroshima,
> In Dallas and Selma too,
> And in South Africa.
>
> We hear you, O Man, in agony cry,
> For freedom you march, in riots you die.
> Your face in the papers we read and we see,
> The tree must be planted by human decree.[11]

Missionary Implications

Cultural differences of the kind we have been describing have posed particularly difficult problems for missionaries. In their attempt to "bring Christ" to people in other cultures, missionaries (and until recently most Christian missionaries were sent from either North America or Europe) sometimes confuse "the gospel" with "the culture," namely, their own.

Charles Kraft, a missionary and professor of missions, recalls an experience in a prescientific culture in Northern Nigeria:

> One day I was presenting the gospel message in the best way I knew how and came to the point where I asserted that the supreme proof that the message of God is true rests in the fact that God raised Jesus Christ from the dead. "Very interesting," one of my hearers replied. "My son rose from the dead just last week, and my uncle last month. My uncle was climbing a tree and he fell out of the tree, died, and, after half an hour, rose from the dead." What does one say to people for whom death and unconsciousness are in the same category?[12]

Culture shock can also flow in the opposite direction. Alice Hageman, a lawyer, Presbyterian minister, and part-time teacher in Cuba, tells of talking with Sergio Arce, professor of theology at the Protestant seminary in Matanzas. When Professor Arce is speaking in North America and Europe, he finds he is often asked, "How is it possible to be a Christian in a communist country?" To which he replies: "How is it possible to be a Christian in a capitalist country?"[13]

Too often in the past missionaries were content simply to export "the gospel" as they knew it. Festus Asana, former principal of the Presbyterian Theological College in Cameroon, reports that "I saw snow for the first time when I left Africa, but years back in Cameroon, during our dry and brown, dusty Christmas season, we would sing:

> In the bleak mid-Winter, Frosty wind made moan,
> Earth stood hard as iron, Water like a stone;
> Snow had fallen, snow on snow, Snow on snow,
> In the bleak mid-winter, Long ago.[14]

And even when the gospel message seems clear, traditions, customs, and unspoken assumptions can alter what the words mean. A former missionary to New Guinea points out how some basic biblical injunctions can be interpreted differently:

> Even such clear statements as the Ten Commandments have, as it were, fuzzy borders. For instance, is it stealing to pick up a child's toy from a suburban sidewalk? Yes, in the United States. No, in Mexico. In ancient Israel one could pick and eat fruit while passing through another man's orchard, but that would be recognized by everyone as theft in present day Southern California. Many Papua New Guineans see my culture's practice of leaving the care of the elderly to the state as a clear violation of the fifth commandment. My Bahinemo [New Guinea] brethren do not see taking a second wife as adultery, but it would be for me. It seems that the essence of each commandment is clear, but the edges are defined differently by different cultures. God's universal standard must be realized in different situations by different behavior.[15]

One solution is to try to sort out what is fundamental to the gospel from what is "merely cultural." But this approach is unsatisfactory, as Kraft discovered when a Nigerian church leader pointed out to him that the Bible commands both that we not steal and that we not allow women to pray with their heads uncovered, and then asked why missionaries teach that the one command be obeyed and the other ignored: are they using a different Bible? In reality both the commands are expressed in terms of customs current in biblical times and places. The solution requires two steps. To understand the original meaning, missionaries (and all Christians) need to look beyond the biblical commands to discover how the words and customs were understood by those who wrote them and those who first heard them. To understand the relevance for today, the missionaries (and all Christians) must also examine the culture we find ourselves in and ask what is God's will in the context of all of the ways God is revealed, through Scripture, tradition, and personal witness.

An even more serious problem is the unconscious assumption on the part of some missionaries that not only is *their* gospel "the gospel," but that their mission is to "bring" it to others by whatever means available. Kraft, who was trained in anthropology as well as theology, describes a situation he encountered in Nigeria:

> I observed in one of my colleagues a disturbing type of behavior that I wanted at all costs to avoid. He took a great interest in the culture of the people he worked among but, when he discovered their secrets, he consistently used this information against them. His attempts to communicate the gospel constantly compared their customs with what he called "the Christian custom." When he described "the Christian custom," however, it always bore a striking resemblance to an idealized version of an American custom.[16]

Then Kraft began to recognize his own cultural biases:

> I, like the majority of my generation of evangelical Protestants, had been taught to fear heresy above almost anything else in the world. I had been taught to respect the nearly two thousand years of Western theological study and to assume that such dedicated theologians had answered just about every problem worth answering....I had been taught to preserve my orthodoxy by closing my mind to other options....I began to realize that, if I were to face the problems of the Nigerian situation squarely, I would have to become more *open* than I had been....I was becoming...open to learning things from people of a different culture concerning what biblical Christianity should look like in their culture. *There was nothing in my church background or theological training that would enable me even to counsel those who were interacting with God in terms of a different culture.* [emphasis supplied][17]

Kraft's insight not only reveals the cultural biases of some missionaries. Even more important, it shows the problem *all* Christians face in understanding the meaning of the gospel in their own cultures today. North American culture has changed radically in the last hundred years. Dress and diet and leisure time activities are strikingly different. And beneath the surface are more crucial changes in the ways we find out about the world, create our assumptions, and make our decisions.

It is the thesis of this book that the mass media of communication have placed Americans in an environment so different from former times that our values, assumptions, perspectives and worldview, and therefore our understanding of religion, are affected at their roots.

The mass media have radically altered the nature of meaning in our lives. This is why Kraft's comment is so apt. Today we live, in effect, in a "different culture" from the culture of thirty years ago, even though we may be still be living in the same place we always did. In a sense, time has speeded up. Since the Second World War we have moved into a new kind of culture — a *mediated* culture, where for the first time in history, whole nations get more of their information and ideas from the mass media than from home, church, and school. We have to learn to understand what this new mediated culture is saying about religious values if we expect to be able to conduct our own quest for meaning within it.

People in North America are "interacting with God in terms of a different culture" — not different in location, but different in terms of the radical transformation that has resulted from the technological revolution. Part of our task is to try to understand the *ways* this technological revolution, and especially the revolution in communications, shapes culture, and it is to that task that we now turn.

3

How Communication Shapes
Our Culture

> Until the lions have their historians, tales of hunting will
> always glorify the hunter.
>
> —African proverb, Oxfam poster, London, 1989

When people tell me that the communication media don't affect
them, I am reminded of the true story of a woman who objected
when a speaker insisted that she probably bought even her toothpaste on the basis of media influence. "What kind of toothpaste
do you buy?" he asked. "Crest," she replied. "But it's not because
of the commercials," she assured him, "it's just that my children
can't brush after every meal!"*

The media do affect us, profoundly. In fact, the history of our
communication technology is, in one sense, also a history of our
cultures: oral, written, printed, and electronic.

We will better understand how the media affect our values and
worldview today if we see in perspective just how much changes
in communication media have affected cultural values throughout
human history.

Oral Communication

We know very little about the first epoch of human history, that
four million years or so when humans lived in an oral mode,

---

*Only those readers under twenty, or who never watch TV, failed to see com-
mercials run throughout the 1970s proclaiming Crest as the toothpaste designed
especially "for those who can't brush after every meal."

because during that period they left almost no records of their existence. From the marvelous cave paintings at Lascaux and elsewhere we know that our forebears were sensitive and articulate people. But because they had not discovered how to arrange written marks in ways to communicate their language, we can know very little about *what* they thought, felt, believed, and valued.

Written Communication

Fairly suddenly, about 3300 B.C., a major change in human communication occurred. Someone, or perhaps some people, invented a system of representing oral speech in *visual* form: writing. At first, pictures stood for things or events. Gradually the pictures were standardized and became symbols or hieroglyphics that could be combined to represent whole new ideas. For example, in Egypt the picture of a river plus a boat meant "travel." Finally alphabets were created, a brilliant leap forward, because with an alphabet a single, finite set of symbols could represent all the *sounds* of speech.

Consider what it meant to be able to *represent what was said*. Marks on clay or papyrus could last for centuries — creating a new sense of history. Letters could be carried from place to place — creating a new understanding of what was "the world." Collections of writings could communicate the ideas of great thinkers — creating new kinds of education. Documents could be carried — creating new kinds of business and trade. Records could be referred to again and again — creating new concepts of truth, of contracts, and of the law.

The invention of writing changed the way people thought. This recognition greatly disturbed some of the early Greeks, who already had a highly developed culture based on the oral tradition. Scholar Eric A. Havelock believes that the transition in Greece from orality to literacy wiped out the need for people to develop a highly accurate memory based on speech, and thus eliminated the need for communicators to express themselves in language that could easily be memorized. The Greek oral tradition — its lengthy sagas, its poetry, its rhythms, its rhymes, its repeats and choruses, its clichés and rich imagery ("brave Odysseus," "fair maiden," "rosy-fingered dawn") — was no longer necessary. The writer was no longer a speaker and therefore no longer needed to concentrate on stories about people; instead, writers were freed to deal more directly with ideas. Thus the new technology of communication was a major factor in the development of Greek philosophy.[1]

In his classic study on *Orality and Literacy*, Walter Ong stresses the importance of writing in the development of human thought. He points out that "orally managed language and thought is not noted for analytic precision." Someone may speak eloquently and present a strong personal presence but express very little in the way of thoughtful ideas. A writer, on the other hand, has no opportunity to use the hand gestures, the facial expressions, the eye contact, the feedback that the speaker enjoys. For this reason the writer must "foresee all possible meanings a statement may have for any possible reader in any possible situation, and you have to make your language work so as to come clear all by itself."[2]

Also, writing *separates* the knower from the known, the writer from the reader. Writing is a solitary activity. It leads to introspection and self-examination. The image of the writer working alone in a solitary garret accurately represents much of written endeavor. In fact, claims Ong, writing "makes possible the great introspective religious traditions such as Buddhism, Judaism, Christianity, and Islam."[3]

Because of the written tradition's fundamental impact upon culture, not all Greeks embraced it gladly. Socrates could not read or write, yet he had fashioned the highest form of oral discourse — at the moment when Greece was changing from oral to written culture. A few years later, Plato, standing on the other side of the line dividing oral from written, was himself profoundly disturbed by the impact of the new technology. In *Phaedrus*, Plato has Socrates comment on writing:

> ...this discovery of yours will create forgetfulness in the learners' souls, because they will not use their memory; they will trust to external written characters and not remember of themselves. The specific which you have discovered is an aid not to memory but to reminiscence, and you give your disciples not truth, but the semblance of truth; they will be hearers of many things and will have learned nothing; they will appear to be omniscient and will generally know nothing; they will be tiresome company, having the show of wisdom without the reality.[4]

Plato understood something about the shift to literacy which we, in our time, must understand about the shift to electronic communication: that communication technologies change not only what we think, but *how*.

Printed Communication

The development of printing again extended our communication environment. While significant, these new changes were not nearly as fundamental as the shift from orality to literacy. Printing was *not* invented by Johann Gutenberg in 1450. In fact, printing was not so much a Western invention as a Western appropriation. The Egyptians had printed books by at least 1350 B.C. There was even a daily newspaper, the *Acta Diurna*, printed on papyrus in Rome in 131, and printed books were sold in Rome throughout the second century A.D. The print was carved on wooden blocks and the blocks were pressed to papyrus a page at a time.

Moveable type, often thought of as the key invention of Gutenberg, actually was in use in China by the eleventh century. In Korea, metal type was first used to print books during the reign of King Kojong in 1250, and moveable metal type was cast "by the thousands" in Korea in 1403 — forty-seven years before Gutenberg.[5]

What Gutenberg did was to mobilize the technology. He created the first *assembly line of interchangeable parts* — the precursor of Henry Ford's automobile factory. From a group of less than thirty characters, Gutenberg made hundreds of "a's," "b's," and "c's," each one of which could be used and reused to create words, and he mounted them on bases that could be fitted together quickly into lines and locked into a frame. He set up six presses, hired twenty-five workmen. It took a great deal of money, three years, and 5,700 calfskins to produce the magnificent Mainz Bible.

Printing was one of the earliest examples of the capitalist spirit. It embodied high technology, assembly line techniques, the separation of the work process into discrete steps, the distancing of the worker from the final product; above all, it proved a highly efficient and therefore highly lucrative business. And it generated a huge new enterprise — the merchandising of books throughout the known world.

Lutheranism grew with the spread of printed books. Between 1517 and 1520, Martin Luther's thirty books and pamphlets sold more than 300,000 copies. Protestantism thoroughly exploited the medium; it was the first movement of any kind to use printing for overt propaganda and agitation against an established institution — the Roman Catholic Church. As Elizabeth Eisenstein says in her book on the role of the printing press, Protestant clergy "viewed printing as a providential device which ended forever a priestly monopoly of learning, overcame ignorance and superstition, pushed back the evil forces commanded by Italian popes, and, in general, brought Western Europe out of the dark ages."[6]

Printing brought ideas, if not to the masses, then at least to the middle classes. Within a few decades, hundreds of thousands of people who could read had access to written works that previously had been accessible only to clergy, teachers, and the very rich. This democratization of learning neatly fit into Luther's emphasis on the priesthood of all believers, Protestantism's view that individuals should make their own decisions about the future of their immortal souls, and the Renaissance insistence that learning and ideas should be available to all. Printing gave a mighty push to the concept that meanings are in people, that ideas get their authority from widespread acceptance, and that individuals should make their own decisions rather than accept those handed down from a higher authority. According to Eisenstein, it was printing, not Protestantism, that finally rendered obsolete Roman Catholic use of the Vulgate Bible, and it was printing, not Protestantism, that set in motion the more democratic and national forms of worship that undermined much of the Roman Catholic Church's control throughout Europe.[7]

But printing also led to enormous dissent within Christendom, setting church leaders at odds with one another. Because various translations of the Bible were so widely available, people could no longer ignore discrepancies in the Scriptures. Some began to question scriptural authorship and to analyze biblical texts in a scholarly way. At the same time, printing allowed religious authorities to demand adherence to "standard" forms of worship, "approved" hymns, and "authorized" biblical texts.

Thus printing had two quite opposite effects on religion. It pushed many Christians toward freedom of thought in relation to authority and toward individual scholarship that ultimately led to the approaches to the Bible called "higher criticism" and "modernism." At the same time, it made possible the spread of more rigid views of right belief, and pushed many Christians toward

dogmatism and later to the approach to doctrine called "fundamentalism."

Electronic Communication

The next leap in communication technology came some five thousand years after the invention of writing, but a mere four hundred
years after the invention of moveable type. Electronic communication comprised a series of inventions that moved us into the
era in which we live.

The speed with which the technology changed is itself astonishing. Consider this listing of major events in the evolution
of communication, and the length of time between significant
changes:

B.C.

4,000,000– 400,000	Human speech
3,500	Writing (Sumer)
1,500	Writing (China)
800	Phonetic alphabet (Phoenicia)

A.D.

131	Block printing (Rome)
450	Block printing (Asia)
1250	Moveable type (Korea)
1456	Moveable type, printing (Germany)
1621	Newspaper (Amsterdam)
1731	Magazine (London)
1839	Photography – Daguerre (France)
1844	Telegraph – Morse (USA)
1858	Cable under the Atlantic – U.K. to Newfoundland
1876	Telephone – Bell (USA)
1877	Phonograph – Edison (USA)
1886	Linotype – Merganthaler (Germany, USA)
1891	Motion pictures – Lumière/Edison (France, USA)
1895	Wireless telegraphy (radio) – Marconi (Italy)
1906	Radio (voice transmission) – Fessendon (Canada, USA)
1920	Radio broadcasting – KDKA Pittsburgh
1923	Television – New York to Philadelphia
1927	Sound movies (USA)
1928	Regular TV broadcast in U.S. – WGY Schenectady
1935	FM radio – Armstrong (USA)

1942   Commercial TV standardized in the U.S.
1946   Electronic computer – University of Pennsylvania
1947   Transistor (AT&T)
1948   TV increases from 100,000 to 1 million sets in USA
1950   Cable TV (USA)
1954   Regular color TV broadcasts (USA)
1957   Global satellite – "Sputnik" (USSR)
1960   Integrated circuit chips (USA)
1983   Operational optical fiber: Boston-Washington[8]

More than *one-half* of all major developments in communication technology have occurred during the last one hundred years.

Of all the electric developments, perhaps the most significant was Samuel F. B. Morse's invention of the telegraph (and the telegraphic code, a whole new alphabet) in 1844. Previously, information could travel no faster than a horse could gallop or a boat could sail. A few attempts had been made to develop line-of-sight signal systems. Napoleon used a string of semaphores on French hill-tops to advantage, and in 1800 a line-of-sight system was opened between Martha's Vineyard and Boston to transmit news from arriving ships. But for all practical purposes, the telegraph brought a fundamental change: information independent of any form of transportation and so fast that *distance was erased.*

Consider some implications. Where the prices of commodities had varied widely from city to city, within a few years after the telegraph, unified national commodity markets could set essentially uniform prices. Where distance from a nation's hub cities — London, Paris, New York — had represented a proportional loss in news, information, and power, now "the provinces" in Europe and North America rapidly increased in economic, social, and political power. Where railroads had been obliged to maintain horses and riders every five miles along the track to race back and forth to warn engineers of impending collisions, the "singing wire" could now control the flow of trains, and not incidentally, their cargoes, so that whole new national distribution systems were possible.

Christians quickly embraced the notion that increased communication would bring about enlightenment and progress, just as sixteenth-century Protestants had seen printing as a providential device to overcome ignorance and superstition and "bring Western Europe out of the dark ages." The telegraph, and the inventions that followed it, gave the multitudes hope for realizing a utopia of universal peace.

But business saw a different potential. James Carey points out that the telegraph was "the first great industrial monopoly," and that its most significant impact was the "relationship between the telegraph and monopoly capitalism."[9] Western Union was the first communication empire, and industrial magnates, including Jay Gould and the Vanderbilt interests, fought to control it. They realized that communication could actively govern physical processes — not only passenger movements, but also railroad stock, production quotas, and distribution schedules. It was not long before a man named Richard B. Sears of North Redwood, Minnesota, combined the railroad, the telegraph, and the new U.S. rural postal system to create a giant new network of merchandising — the mail order house. When he joined forces with Mr. Roebuck, the Sears-Roebuck Catalogue quickly became a household staple, symbolically and literally replacing the family Bible in thousands of living rooms across America.

"Wireless" radio extended communication to ships at sea and across continents, and undersea cables brought about whole new kinds of communication with other continents. Thoreau feared the new cable technology would merely trivialize the news, bringing us word "that Princess Adelaide has the whooping cough."[10] It did. But it also extended Britain's sinews of power, allowing it to consolidate its empire in India, Burma, and Kenya.

Meanwhile, commercial radio succeeded in galvanizing whole nations around a new kind of experience: professionally produced stories, musicals, and immediate news — all designed for the ear. At the same time, faster and more centralized communication enlarged the power of big-city newspapers; at the turn of the century their muckraking reporters captured the popular imagination with crusades against corruption and fraud. Soon even faster presses and better paper made possible a whole new kind of news reporting: photo journalism. And where such serialized magazine writers as Charles Dickens and Edgar Allen Poe had captured the imagination of nineteenth-century readers with their latter-day morality plays carried in *Harpers Bazaar* and other periodicals, now such new slick-paper magazines as *Liberty, Saturday Evening Post*, and *Colliers* provided color versions of those same morality tales to twentieth-century readers. The culminating point was reached by *LIFE* magazine, which documented in photo essay form the life and times of the Western world during the forties and fifties.

Then beginning about 1950, television brought it all together. TV had radio's immediacy and reach into every home. It had the picture magazine's ability to encapsule events in pictures. It had the movies' ability to tell stories. Television could go anywhere, cover anything. It could speed events up and slow them down. It could magnify the atom and miniaturize the world. It could speak to us, tell us stories, be with us — any time of the day or night.

Yes, the nature of communication technology has always had a major effect on culture. Yet technology only produces tools; it is up to human beings to decide *how* to incorporate those tools into the culture. Therefore, the question we need to answer next is: how is the new communication technology being used? By whom? For what purposes? With what social and personal effects? And how does the use of the media shape what has meaning and value in our time?

4

How Culture Shapes
Our Meanings

"Greed works."
–Michael Douglas in the film *Wall Street*

The Spirit of Capitalism

The new technologies of electronic communication have taken on
a central, dominant role in our culture. But why? Why have TV
and radio and film achieved such success in our society? After all,
technologies flourish only if they are useful in society.

For example, about the time color TV came on the market,
General Electric also came out with the oven hoods that contained electric exhaust fans. For thirty years the electric oven hood
has sold an average of less than a few hundred thousand units
a year, while today almost every household in the United States
and Canada owns at least one color TV set — more than one hundred million sets — and about five million sets are sold annually.[1]
What made the difference? Simply that our North American culture could hardly function as we know it today without color TV,
while the loss of the electric oven hood would scarcely be missed.
In other words, the mass media did not simply impose themselves
upon our culture: *something* in the culture itself needed what the
mass media of communication could supply.

As I have studied the mass media and their effects for many
years, I have come to believe that the formative power that made
mass communication technology both possible and powerful was
the development of industrial capitalism. Capitalism, beginning in

its industrialized form about two hundred years ago, was ⌐ thing radically new in the history of the world. Growing ovᴄ the previous two centuries out of the Renaissance and Reformation focus on the individual, and building momentum from new economic ventures, new markets, and new industrialization, its fundamental values were pragmatism and technology. Its measure of success was efficiency. Its method was standardization. It asked only "does it work?" not "what, or whom, does it work *for*?"

In order for standardization to work, everything — including people — had to be fragmented, that is, divided into components that could be put together quickly, cheaply, and with as little attention to individual differences as possible — as in printing. This process affected everything in our society, but especially the way we communicate. With standardization came fragmentation, separation. Cultural historian John Staudenmaier believes that capitalism tends to separate people's inner selves from their outward "persona," that is, the self they project to others. It tends to separate news and information from their context, so that we find it difficult to connect bits and pieces of information in ways that make sense to us. And it tends to separate those who shape public mass media messages from their audience, so that we cannot easily judge whether the writer or speaker is "real" or trustworthy.[2]

Capitalism is not just an economic theory of infusing profits into businesses to produce more goods. It also brings with it an ideology, which Staudenmaier believes is essentially antihuman:

> The frightening invention of capitalism is not the creation of artificial or new needs. The terrible invention is the concept that there is such a thing as purely physical or biological need. Other social systems had treated human beings as social entities, not biological machines. Only capitalism...conceived of human beings as raw material.[3]

An interesting example of capitalism's determination to standardize *people* was the development, beginning in the 1830s, of the etiquette book. At that time waves of new immigrants were arriving in the cities of North America, and etiquette books emerged which taught these newcomers, who would become middle-class citizens, how to avoid misbehaving in public. Society's leaders saw etiquette books as valuable ways to manage

..ass; its readers saw them as a valuable way to
..adder. Here, for example, is advice from an 1889
:cess in Society:

..k behind you in the street, or behave in any way
s.......attract attention. Do not talk or laugh loudly out
of doo.s, or swing your arms as you walk. If you should
happen to meet someone you know, take care not to utter
their names loudly.[4]

Today's "etiquette manuals," such as *House Beautiful*, *Woman's Day*, *Cosmopolitan*, *Playboy*, and *Field and Stream*, continue to tell us how to dress our selves and our homes, how to play and work, how to treat our children and friends, and, above all, how to act in order to be a "success in society." Today's other "etiquette manual" is, of course, television.

A hundred and fifty years ago, the demands for conformity and standardization were most pressing in the area of industrial production. In 1815 the U.S. Ordnance Department standardized its weapons production, which set in motion a revolution in all production values. Not only was the Winchester repeating rifle a cheap and efficient way to subdue the Indians, but its interchangeable parts were the harbinger of new ways to produce and move goods of all kinds.

Consider, for example, how grain transportation changed radically during the 1860s. In St. Louis, following the old system, grain was bagged, loaded onto train cars, then offloaded at the edge of town where the tracks ended, carried by wagon across the city, and then loaded onto river boats. By contrast, in Chicago a new design allowed the grain to be bulk loaded into cars because the company owned tracks all the way to the docks, where the grain was bulk loaded onto grain boats. Historian J. L. Larson points out that the Chicago system was far more efficient, but it also eliminated the ability of the small operators — the loaders, the cart drivers, and so on — to negotiate their own contracts, and thus to maintain their livelihood:

If the Chicago system was a model of integration, speed, and efficiency, the St. Louis market preserved the integrity of each man's transaction and employed a host of small entrepreneurs at every turn — real virtues in ante-bellum America.[5]

The new capital-intensive standardized system in Chicago eliminated many of the variables — human negotiations — and increased profits much more rapidly. It was, in terms of the rapidly developing cultural value of efficiency, a very "successful" system, though hundreds of small operators lost their jobs.

Control of all components of society became even more important for a profitable business climate as we moved into the twentieth century. Social scientists began to write about the importance of social management. For example, in 1889 sociologist Edward Alsworth Ross urged "the right persons [that is, social scientists] to undertake the study of moral influences...in the right spirit as a basis for the scientific control of the individual."[6]

Ross warned that scientists who undertook this task must not reveal their scientific secrets, because "to betray the secrets of social ascendancy is to forearm the individual in his struggle with society."[7]

Individual creativity tends to disrupt the smooth functioning of a large production system, and the investment of large amounts of capital in production requires procedures that will minimize risk and maximize profits. Thus Henry Ford could raise the capital necessary to produce the epitome of the mass production system only after he designed an assembly line. First identical parts were manufactured; then they were assembled in sequence by identical workers who each attached only a single part and who were otherwise completely isolated from the process. Ford's assembly line produced a car that could be purchased in only one style and in any color — so long as it was black. It produced workers who contributed nothing creative to the production and who got no joy out of it, except for their paycheck at the end of the week.

Capitalism's Shaping of Communication

But industrial production and transportation were not the only parts of culture transformed by the spirit of capitalism. Communication was affected perhaps more than other aspects of society, because the new communication technologies were the key not only to production but also to the distribution and consumption of those products.

Consider the transformation of news. Before Morse's telegraph, almost all news was local. The town crier and the local newspaper writers lived among their audiences. When news came from out of town, it often was accompanied by visitors who, as they delivered a newspaper or magazine, could say, "But I was there, and it was not like that; it was more like this."

Electronic communication quickly separated source from audience. Soon local newspapers were *buying* "news" written by anonymous writers in centralized agencies in the big cities. A small town paper in Iowa could get this newly created, purchased news almost as quickly as those in the cities — but without personal contact. The system that wire made possible was largely a one-way system. The audience no longer was able to interact with the story writers and town criers were no more. The audience became totally passive.

Also, when "news" became a commodity, its content changed. There had to be news to sell every day, whether or not something newsworthy had happened. The newspaper had to be run as an efficient business, selling advertising and appealing to readers (who were now customers) every day. So news had to be interesting enough to persuade the local editor to purchase it on a regular basis, and its entertainment value became more and more important. It had to be fast — faster than the locals could get it elsewhere, or it was worthless. Thus news became transformed from the old story-telling format to an endless conveyor belt of disconnected items. Its priority was to interest as many readers as possible, and immediacy counted far more than accuracy or thoughtful background and perspective.

Radio began in the early 1920s and almost immediately became a commercial enterprise in the United States. While Canada had a mix of public and private radio, as early as 1929 "the majority of programmes heard [were] from sources outside of Canada," namely, the U.S.[8] Radio took the immediacy of news one step further. Now the audience could "participate" in events "as they happened." But the impression of "being there" was actually based on events carefully selected for their ease of coverage, their universal appeal, and their simplicity. Radio provided an illusion of "knowing" about an event when in reality the audience was given no chance at all to question the situation, to participate in discussion, or to hear a wide diversity of opinions about it. In other words, listeners experienced fragmented communication — little pieces of information supplied with very little context, background, or perspective. Just as the demands of production had fragmented people into interchangeable jobs and skills that fit the system, so the demands of communication to "reach" people in the mass further fragmented their understanding, yet without touching them in their wholeness as persons. Now even people's *ideas* were fragmented.

With the coming of television, people were further encouraged to meet the needs of capitalism: to consume without end, to use up, throw away, and buy again; to repress individuality so as not to question the process which provided an endless stream of products; to seek the immediate and the sensational, changing the channel every few seconds if it did not provide immediate stimulation; and, above all, never to ask questions about the real *meaning* of the system itself.

Sylvester (Pat) Weaver, president of NBC-TV in the early 1950s, was one of the first to recognize the true nature of television. In 1955 he told a group of advertising executives that the automation in post–World War II factories required exactly what television could provide:

> ... the automated business needs a constant, dependable, un-fluctuating demand for its output.... This and other solutions to steady demand mean a new kind of selling — a complete change in emphasis — educational selling to wean consumers from old habits.... That instrument — *the greatest mutation in communications history* ... man's greatest communications invention — television. A medium that proved itself, from the first, to be also the most powerful, exciting, flexible of all advertising media.[9]

Yes, television and the whole new commercial media environment was a great success, but *what was the measure of "success"?*

We have briefly sketched how our culture interacted with the new technologies during the last century and a half, producing a new culture based on the technologies. The technologies have "cultivated" the culture, and the culture has appropriated the technologies. To see how this acculturation process works and how the spirit of capitalism has succeeded in influencing our lives through communication, let us look at examples in two rather unlikely situations: an amusement park and the national space race.

Disneyland as Moral Educator

In August 1965, Nikita Khrushchev accepted an invitation from President Nixon to tour the United States. It was the first time a Russian head of state had been on U.S. soil. Khrushchev impressed the American public with his wit, warmth, humanness, and nerve, but he also confounded everyone by his insistence that, above all, he wanted to visit Disneyland.

Since it opened in July 1955, Disneyland in Anaheim, California, and its later clone, Walt Disney World near Orlando, Florida, have been hosts to more Americans, and probably to more human beings, than any other single "event" in history. Each park boasts several "lands," scores of attractions, dozens of food facilities and more than fifty shops, employs three to seven thousand people depending on the season, and entertains about ten thousand people on an average day.

Why was the premier of the Union of Soviet Socialist Republics determined to see Disneyland? Because Disneyland is the American Dream, the American Way, and when one has been there, one has experienced a unique distillation of our values and our worldview. Disneyland is a gigantic sales machine of American culture. And as Walt Disney himself explained to Lloyd Shearer on a tour when Disneyland first opened in 1955, it sells just one product:

> What I'm trying to sell here in Anaheim is what everyone wants, happiness. You can call it corn or cotton candy or escape, or anything you want. But to me I'm selling happiness.
>
> Now, what's most conducive to happiness? Simply a pleasant experience in the company of happy, smiling, friendly people.... If this park ever becomes successful, and everyone tells me it's gonna fall flat on its face, it won't be because we keep it clean and don't sell gum or because we provide great fun and games — it will be because our personnel sincerely sell happiness. Hell! That's what we all want, isn't it? A little bit of happiness![10]

Every major civilization envisions some kind of utopia that it feels constitutes the ideal life. The early Hebrews had the Garden of Eden. The Greeks had Plato's Republic, and early Christendom had Augustine's City of God. St. Francis, St. Dominic, and

St. Benedict proposed whole environments, monastic orders that attempted to express the ideal living condition. In early America several settlements, including New Salem, the Shaker communities, and the early Mormon towns, were based on views of the ideal life.

Today Disneyland performs the same function. Disneyland has become a kind of utopia, a vision of the ideal life for twentieth-century Americans, a place where pilgrims from every corner of the nation and world assemble, bringing the whole family, a place to which they often return, again and again, throughout their lifetime.

Disneyland is divided into several "lands," all of them accessible through Main Street, which provides an avenue of transition from the reality of traffic jams, smog and vast car parks to the fantasies of clean, orderly and non-threatening Adventureland, Tomorrowland, and Frontierland. But Main Street is itself fantasy, as Walt Disney explains:

> It's not apparent at a casual glance that this street is only a scale model. We had every brick and shingle and gas lamp made seven-eighths size. This costs more, but made the street a toy, and the imagination can play more freely with a toy. Besides, people like to think their world is somehow more grown up than Papa's was.[11]

Main Street leads to Tomorrowland, which boasts a vision of the future as envisioned by "America's foremost men of science and industry," according to Disney.[12] The exhibits are in fact provided by some of America's largest corporations — General Electric, American Telephone and Telegraph, Monsanto, and so on — and generally extol the virtues of technological progress while familiarizing people with the latest gadgets developed by industry. The constantly repeated message is: "technology is *good* for you," and never mind the problems of environmental pollution, decaying inner cities, homeless thousands, or poverty-stricken millions.

Fantasyland fulfills its name. It comes right out of Disney's film productions, a place where we meet animated "real-life" versions of goodness personified (Snow White, the third Little Pig, Dumbo, Pollyanna) and the essence of evil (the Wicked Queen, the Big Bad Wolf) — and thus learn to divide the world into good and evil, watching goodness triumph with a smile and a song.

Frontierland is less childish. It is built around scenes of conquest — conquest over the American frontier, the American Indian, and over nature itself. But the stories of Davy Crockett, forts, and Indian attacks bear little resemblance to history and its real people. For example, culture analyst Michael Real notes that "mechanically reconstructed animals and plants in the Nature's Wonderland part of Frontierland stand out as an antithesis to the sensitivity to nature maintained in real life by Native Americans."[13]

While from an individual perspective Disneyland offers pure fantasy, from a cultural perspective its mythmaking — the stories and environmental settings — provide powerful indoctrination. In any culture, the most dangerous communications are those that we do not take seriously. And if we add to the equation the great technical skill which Disneyland's managers focus on every aspect of our experience, we have awesome communication indeed. Michael Real evaluates the overall "message" of Disneyland:

> Disney's ethical dramas seem to serve the "civil religion" of America, which combines the strains of the Puritan theocrats and the republican Founding Fathers. Disney presentations lack the "ultimacy" necessary to be considered religious. Nevertheless, to the rootless youth of southern California, Disney becomes an important reality-adjusting mechanism: the Disney universe offers a larger-than-life ground and source of beliefs about life and people and society.[14]

Khrushchev was right to visit Disneyland. What better place could one go to understand American culture? And have fun at the same time?

Merchandising the Moon

Cultural myths and values are sold to us not through recreation alone; they also are sold through information. Perhaps the most significant, and most successful, information-selling process of the second half of our century was the selling of science and technology through the American space program.

"That's one small step for a man; one giant leap for mankind!" When Neil Armstrong uttered this epigram and implanted the first footprint on the moon in July 1969, the impression seen instantly by hundreds of millions of persons was unforgettable.

But that event, while dramatic, only crowned twelve years of careful indoctrination managed by a remarkable marriage of two of the most powerful forces in American society: the military-industrial complex, which needed to generate a national fixation on the wonders of science and technology in order to sell the Congress and public on ever-greater expenditures; and the mass-media news and information complex, which needed the drama and scope of a race to the moon to capture the millions of viewers necessary to sell commercial time-slots to advertisers.

It was a marriage made, if not in heaven, then surely in the USA, because at the time these two institutions were uniquely American. Since the development of the atomic bomb and its deployment at Hiroshima and Nagasaki in 1945, the United States had held undisputed worldwide dominance in both military and industrial prowess. At the same time American advertising had grown into the single most powerful element of the burgeoning American production and consumption cycle.

It was only natural that these two giants should find common interests. In some ways the selling of technology, especially military technology, began with the dropping of the first atom bomb. We now know that in 1945 the creation of the *image* of the atomic bomb was as important to the decision makers as its actual military effect. That summer, with Germany already defeated and the cities of Japan in flames, the Target Committee appointed by President Truman discussed whether or not to drop the bomb. In recommending a "go" to the president they stressed "(1) obtaining the greatest psychological effect against Japan and (2) making the initial use sufficiently spectacular for the importance of the weapon to be internationally recognized when publicity on it was released."[15] Here the government was beginning to understand what the business community had long known: that it is just important to sell the image of the device as the device itself.

In fact, selling the space race was not fundamentally different from selling next year's new automobile. The automobile industry had learned a great deal about selling during the first half of the century. When Henry Ford merchandized his Model T shortly after World War I, advertising was based on the assumption that the seller and buyer were equally accessible, equally knowledgeable, equally powerful. So Henry advertised the intrinsic *quality* of the product itself: his cars were relatively inexpensive, ran well, were easy to fix, and lasted a long time.

But as mass-produced goods of all kinds continued to flood the market, advertising began to change. Its objective became how to motivate people to buy more and more of the impersonally produced, impersonally sold goods — without losing the "personal" touch. In 1919 Henry was selling Fords in a society where 90 percent of the populace had never owned a car. But by 1923, he faced a radically new situation: 90 percent of his potential buyers already owned a car. Yet the production-consumption cycle had to go on. The solution arrived in the person of Alfred P. Sloan, president of General Motors. Sloan recognized that advertising must take a radically new course. It must convince people to identify *who they are* with *what they own*, to be dissatisfied with what they have, and to believe that new is better. These were the essential new myths. If the public bought these myths, they could be sold anything — including a new car — whether they needed it or not. Thus GM products, using the new advertising approach, made great strides during the late twenties and early thirties simply by changing the styling, adding push-buttons for windshield wipers and ventilation, and giving the public a choice of colors and chrome trim.

In addition, advertising learned to deal with the fantasy life of its audience. To stay with the automobile illustration, cars no longer were merchandized as transportation machines but were sold primarily as extensions of the *self* — symbols of power, sexual drive, freedom, and status. However, the machine aspect was still important, and advertising for next year's models was filled with encouragement about horsepower, power transmissions, overdrive, and other quasi-technical jargon — all designed to convince the potential owner that he (and most auto ads of the period were blatantly sexist) was in charge of something powerful, something amenable to his will and control. They sold the sizzle, not the steak.

The conquest of space simply built upon these bedrock principles of the emerging advertising industry. The mythmakers went to work. The space ship was itself an example of man (sic) conquering the new frontier — space itself. The astronauts (a word coined for the occasion, and richly evocative of the sailors and adventurers of Greek myths) were chosen amid a blaze of publicity. Out of all five hundred or so military pilots in the entire United States, only a few dozen were selected for the final tests, and of those only the famous Seven were chosen. All were white, from middle-American small towns, and had typical "American" families. We soon got to know John Glenn, Buzz Aldrin, and Neil Armstrong better than we knew most of the people living on our block, thanks to nonstop television coverage of their lives, families, training, successes, and problems. Advertising well understood the importance of personalizing the product, and the space race was no exception.

Present, too, was the emphasis upon *manned* flight. While the USSR's space program depended much more on automated flight, the U.S. program emphasized *control* by humans — even though in reality all John Glenn could do was peer through a tiny window during most of his flight, while computers and ground signals managed the actual controls. The space program also depended upon another automobile innovation: the unveiling. Where new car models had been carefully concealed to hype consumer interest and then unveiled in a blaze of lights (or in carefully staged "spy" photos), the latest rockets, boosters, and command capsules were unveiled at Cape Kennedy amid even greater blazes of light and hype.

Finally, NASA knew the importance of education along with ballyhoo, and a huge Space Center was erected at Cape Kennedy (just a few miles from Disney World) where families could see a super-wide-screen movie celebrating the technological marvels of the space program, tour actual rockets and historic space capsules, and on occasion even see a blast-off of one of the many space launches. Added to this, of course, were millions of copies of various readers made available to public schools for the edification of children, and Sunday supplements with the same information, adult-style, for their parents.

The message of the selling of the moon was simply that technology is the most powerful force in human affairs and that the United States is "ahead in the space race." It can scarcely be underestimated how important it was that Americans accept this mythology. It was the engine that moved Congress to allocate enormous sums to maintain the wealth and power of the military-industrial complex. It motivated a change in public school curriculum during the 1950s and beyond toward science, mathematics, and engineering at the expense of history, communication skills, and the liberal arts. It supplied the mythology that fed a magical belief in the ultimate power of science, or rather, of scientism and technology, which to many people amounted to the same thing.

Culture changes as people try to orient themselves in their world and to explain to themselves "what's going on." It changes even more under the influence of a strong ideology. For most nations in the Western world in our time, the prevailing economic ideology is capitalism. But capitalism influences far more than economics; it profoundly influences the total culture. Our culture and its communication modes have changed more during the last century and a half than in any other period in cultural history. In this time of advanced capitalism, the mass media sells etiquette books, interchangeable jobs, packaged news, and everything from automobiles to satellites — all to meet the demands of technologies and worldviews that work best with standardization and conformity.

We have hinted at some of the values and worldviews embedded within this culture in which we find ourselves. Let us explore these more directly, and see how they compare and contrast with the values and worldview of people who call themselves Christian — those who try to relate to the values and worldview of the gospel.

5

Worldviews in Conflict

And he asked them, "But who do *you* say that I am?"
                                    –Mark 8:29; Luke 9:20

We may discover that the media reveal more about ourselves and
our culture than we really want to know. Today's mass media
are the windows of our culture. They provide the myths — the
stories and images — that explain to us who we are, what we can
do, what we *cannot* do, who as nations we once were and who
we can be — in other words, the worldview that explains, unites,
and guides our lives.

    To uncover the media's worldview, we have to look for the
symbolic meanings behind the news stories, the situation come-
dies, the movies and commercials. Here, underlying myths reveal
much more than do surface story lines, "messages," or "content."
The myths determine what has meaning, including the meaning
of social roles in the society — who has the power, who is the
aggressor, who is the victim. They tell us "the way things are."
In the media these myths are like the rules of speech: we take
them for granted but they control much of what we can say, how
we say it, and therefore how and what we think.

    Like gravity, air, and mother love, the media's myths are
givens, the "rules behind the rules"; it doesn't occur to us to
question or try to change them. In the aggregate they summarize the worldview in which we operate. We will see that the
media's worldview is quite different from the worldview of Christians, or indeed of the worldviews of all truly religious people.
The differences have resulted in a conflict of worldviews; how

that conflict is resolved will determine what kind of world our children's children will live in.

Myths About the Media

To get a fix on the media's worldview, let us look first at four myths about the media themselves. These myths supply the context and situation in which the communication exists. Here are four basic myths about the media — assumptions about communication that are never stated as such but are present in almost every media presentation.

1. *The media tell us the way life really is.* Despite the fantasies which pour out of mass media, there is an accompanying underlying assumption that the media have an inherent validity. Partly this claim rests on the mass audience feeling that because something is duplicated in millions of homes, it must be true, or at least "real." Researchers tell us that when people in the 1989 San Francisco earthquake recovered from the shock of feeling the earth move, in many cases their next act was to turn on television, because they needed to have their real-life experience validated by the media. There is something about seeing and hearing, while knowing that millions of others are seeing and hearing the same thing, that allowed Walter Cronkite, for example, to claim at the conclusion of his newscast, "And that's the way it is...."

2. *Information overload is inevitable.* The media also carry the myth that the tremendous avalanche of words, sounds, and visual images that invades our lives through the media is part of the price we must pay for living in modern society. If we expect to benefit from the wide variety of audiovisual experiences now available, the media tell us that we have to expect the demands, sales pitches, commercials, and sheer volume that issue from them.

3. *The issues of life are simple.* Since we live in a world full of information overload, it is necessary and possible to reduce everything really worth knowing into simple good and bad. The media help us identify who and what is "good" and "bad," whether we should respond "yes" or "no" to a particular issue or situation.

4. *There exists a free flow of information.* Of course the whole import of this book's analysis is that instead of a genuinely free flow of information, consistent, pervasive, and effective selection, rearrangement, and censorship are applied to both content and style in the mass media. Such a view is resisted most of all by the

men and women who spend their careers reporting the news in the media. But they are the very ones least able to judge the matter, for they were selected and trained by the system so that they could be depended upon to operate within its assumptions and myths. When was the last time you saw a woman in her sixties or a man with a definite Hispanic accent anchoring the evening TV news? Although the examples may seem farfetched, the point is not; viewpoints and perspectives that are alien to the existing power structure have almost no opportunity to find authoritative expression in mass media.

The Cultural Worldview

There are also media myths about the society in general, and taken together these myths constitute the total cultural worldview. In a complex society such as ours, it would be impossible to detail all of the images and symbols that go into creating its myths. However, here are five of the central myths from which many of the media images and symbols spring.[1]

1. *Efficiency is the highest good.* This assumption of the spirit of capitalism is that solving problems, "getting things done," being more efficient is the primary human goal. Everything else, including other human goals and values, is secondary. The right question is "How can we solve this problem right now?" not, "What is our ultimate objective and how do we reach it?" The ultimate objective *is* efficiency, and whatever gets something "done" (never mind in relation to what) is good.

2. *Technology defines society.* Technology is progress, and progress is simply inevitable: it cannot be stopped, regardless of the human implications. Technology thus takes on a reality that is beyond human influence. Society does not decide how to use technology; technology decides how society will be used.

3. *The fittest survive.* According to sociologist Marie Augusta Neal, a major myth of our Western culture is the concept of "social Darwinism," the theory propounded by Herbert Spencer in the nineteenth century that the principles of biological evolution can be applied to human societies. This myth proposes that actual genetic differences exist between ethnic groups or social classes, differences distinctive enough that society is justified in allowing "more naturally capable" groups to be responsible for making the decisions that affect everyone. Social Darwinism operates in our policy making regarding education, jobs, housing, zoning, provi-

sions for recreation, health services, and the uses of human beings
to carry on wars.

It is no accident that in the Gerbner TV-violence profile, lower-
class and nonwhite characters are depicted as especially prone to
victimization, as more violent than their middle-class counterparts,
as paying a high price for engaging in violence (jail, death).[2] As
this myth suggests, the fittest survive, and the fittest in our media
worldview are *not* poor and nonwhite Americans.

4. *Power and decision making start at the center and move out.*
In the media world, the political word comes from Washington,
the financial word comes from New York, and the entertainment
word comes from Hollywood. While watching television, one gets
the sense of existing at the edge of a giant web in which someone at the center pulls the right string and instantaneously millions of us "out there" see what it has been decided that we will
see.

Of course, one of the early documents of democracy, the U.S.
Declaration of Independence, proposed just the opposite — that
government derives its power from the consent of the governed,
in other words, that power should flow from the periphery to the
center. But the center-out model is much more supportive of the
needs of the industrial revolution, the rise of major nation-states,
and the demands of the new technological era. Center-out clearly
is essential to the maintenance of both centralized governmental
bureaucracies and capitalist economies.

5. *Happiness consists of limitless material acquisition.* This myth
has several corollaries.

One is that *consumption is inherently good* — a concept driven
home effectively by the advertising industry. Another is that *property, wealth, and power are more important than people.* To see how
far this myth has made its way into our consciousness, we need
only consider the vast following for Ronald Reagan's proposition
that the Panama Canal is "ours" because "we" bought and paid
for it. The U.S. did, after all, build the Canal. The fact that U.S.
control of the Canal Zone today deprives the people of Panama
of their human rights is regrettable — but a deal is a deal. Or recall the riots in some U.S. urban ghettos during the late 1960s.
It was when looters started to take things from the stores that
the police started to kill. Both human life and property may be
sacred, but, in the media worldview, property rights are just a little more sacred. Consider this myth in terms of the demands of

third-world nations to be forgiven part of their crushing deb⸗ first-world banks.

Finally, what are the values that the mass media communicate to us on behalf of our culture? *Power* heads the list: power over others; power over nature. As Hannah Arendt pointed out, in today's media world it is not so much that power corrupts as that the aura of power, its glamorous trappings, attracts.[3] Close to power are the values of *wealth* and *property*, the idea that *everything can be purchased* and that *consumption* is an intrinsic good. The values of *narcissism*, of *immediate gratification* of wants, and of *creature comforts* follow close behind.

Thus the mass media worldview tells us that we are basically good, that happiness is the chief end of life, and that happiness consists in obtaining material goods. The media transform the value of sexuality into sex appeal, the value of self-respect into pride, the value of will-to-live into will-to-power. They exacerbate acquisitiveness into greed; they deal with insecurity by generating more insecurity, and anxiety by generating more anxiety. They change the value of recreation into competition and the value of rest into escape. And perhaps worst of all, the media constrict our experience and substitute media world for real world so that we become less and less able to make the fine value judgments that living in such a complex world requires.

Within society, the media are the obedient servants of the economic system. The high technology required for our current mass communication system, with its centralized control, its high profits, its capital-intensive nature, and its ability to reach every individual in the society immediately and economically, makes it perfectly suited for a massive production-consumption system that is equally centralized, profitable, and capital-intensive. In fact, our current first-world production-consumption system simply could not *exist* without a communication system that trains people to be knowledgeable, efficient, and hard-working producers and consumers. The fact that capitalism tends to turn everything into a commodity is admirably suited to the myths of the mass media which turn each member of the audience into a consumer.

In terms of the political system, the media, again reflecting the values held by society generally, give us politics by image, treating politicians and their campaigns as products to be sold rather than as people and ideas to be understood. The whole media approach to the U.S. war in Vietnam was guided by the necessity

r to create for itself an image that would convince
ad itself — that it was number one, the mightiest
1. More recently, the U.S. invasion of Grenada and
f Libya were handled the same way to support the

The way he media handled Watergate is revealing in this regard. The public and the media were shocked not so much by what the president and his men *did* as by the fact that they got caught, publicly, in a way that could not be "imaged" away. But after Watergate we saw an immediate return to the old value system. Those indicted and convicted were overwhelmed with lucrative offers from publishers and television to tell their stories, thus once again driving home the point that society demands "positive" images, including even more lies and fabrications, in order to mitigate the horror of the coverup, to rehabilitate the criminals in the American TV viewer's eyes, and, above all, to help restore, through imagery, the public's confidence in the political system.

The Christian Worldview

Christianity has its own worldview, its own vision of who people are and are not, of what they can and cannot do, and what is of value and what is not. The calling of Christians has always been to evaluate and understand the historical order in terms of the eternal order, to learn how to live within the present world and yet not be of it, to discern both the signs of the times and the signs of God's reign. But to fulfill this calling today requires understanding and evaluating the current media, and television in particular, from a Christian perspective. It requires theological analysis.

I am not overstating the case to say that theological analysis of media is an essential task for North American Christians today. People need to cultivate the ability to stand back enough to gain aesthetic and intellectual "distance" between themselves and what they see in the media, and then, from a critical perspective informed by their own faith, to look at what the media are doing and saying.

Unless we can achieve and maintain this "distance," we easily become victims of our own ignorance and complacency. The world of television quickly becomes our only world. On the other hand, if people develop a stance of critical reflection, they can both clarify their own value system and search for the roots of their faith. This moving back and forth between faith and practice, between spirit and reality, between the realm of God and the realms of this world, is precisely the calling of all who today consider themselves religious.

Theological analysis of this sort is not really so difficult. It is rooted in the Bible, in the history of the church, and in personal reflection. And it certainly is too important to be left to the professional theologians! What it requires is a reasonable amount of biblical literacy and a determination to be completely honest.

The place to begin is with the great themes of the Bible:[4]

The creation story. The Hebrew Scriptures begin with an affirmation of the goodness of God's creation ("...and God saw that it was good"). The Genesis creation narrative reaches its climax in God's creation of man and woman, making it clear that we are not self-produced, independent beings, but creatures — parts of the whole of creation. Genesis thus affirms the fundamental value of each human life, our essential equality as human beings, and our interrelatedness with nature. It demands that we be good *stewards* of creation, rather than its exploiters. Genesis also reminds us forcibly that sin is an inescapable part of human life, and that sin has its roots in our determination to do what we want to do rather than to live in harmony with the world as God wants us to live. This view of creation stands in sharp contrast to our culture's frequent affirmation of consumption and waste, and the media's view that our nature is to consume — to use up and exploit both people and things and to dominate all of creation.

The fall. The recognition that evil can come into the world through the self-centeredness of individuals is a strong corrective to the media's frequent appeals to narcissism, to self-glorification and instant gratification. But sin also appears when the bonds of community and the sense of mutual responsibility are broken, when people lose their sense of self-worth; this understanding of the fallen state strongly judges the media's tendency to fragment community and to separate people from each other.

The covenant story. Even when the human world plunges itself into sin, God does not give up. Reconciliation takes place after the fall, after alienation and pride and selfishness have separated humanity from God's will. God' blessing of Abraham and Sarah and their descendants affirms that God will be with all humanity if they worship the true God and not other less-than-God gods. This means that the worship of *anything* that is less than God —

possessions, power, beauty, success — is a sin. Yet these are the very things glorified (worshipped?) in the mythology of television.

The reign of God. Jesus taught that the reign of God is within us (or among us) — it is not something "out there." It is present in the Spirit, waiting for women and men to testify to its presence and power in their lives. It also is present in hope for the future, in the expression of that toward which we are called to strive in the face of seemingly impossible odds in the real world. The media, on the other hand, propose a world in which value is "out there," in things external to people. Media tell people that the value of people consists in what they own, but that they can never own enough.

The servant and Savior. Jesus is both servant and Savior, who through his death and resurrection becomes the Lord of history, providing both reconciliation and hope for us all. This key image guides both the Christian's personal life and the church's life. The television image is that consumption is the guide to both personal and corporate life, that the priority task for each individual is to "look out for number one."

Several specific values emerge from this biblical view. Through Amos God calls for justice and righteousness (Amos 5:21–24). Through Micah God requires kindness and humility (Micah 6:8). And through Isaiah God demands that we correct oppression (Isaiah 42–43).

Instead of the media's affirmation of wealth and possessions, Jesus tells the rich young ruler to sell all that he has and to follow his way. He makes it clear that wealth has the same chance of entering the kingdom of God as a rope has of threading a needle (Luke 18:18–23).

As for the media's assumption that money can buy anything, Jesus tells the story of the wealthy farmer who decided to build a bigger barn, but then suddenly died, so Jesus asks, "What does one gain by winning the whole world at the cost of one's true self?" (Mark 8:36, NEB).

In contrast to the media's affirmation of the ultimate value of creature comforts and self-gratification, Jesus affirms that anyone who wants to be a follower must leave self-centeredness behind and follow him, which involves taking up the cross (Matt. 16:24).

In contrast to the media's urging us to look out for number one, the Christian worldview urges us to love our enemies.

In contrast to the media's emphasis on power that begins at

the center and moves out, Jesus *begins* with the pc
powerless.

In contrast to the media's tendency to fragment
people, the Christian worldview encourages the value of creating
and maintaining a community of faith in which everyone can be
a part.

In contrast to the media's worldview that we are basically
good, that happiness is the chief end of life and that happiness consists of obtaining material goods, the Christian worldview
holds that human beings are susceptible to the sin of pride, that
the chief end of life is to live in harmony with all of creation,
and that happiness consists in creating the reign of God within
one's self and among one's neighbors — which includes the whole
earth.

Implications

In the first five chapters of this book we have analyzed the universal search for meaning, and in particular the Christian's search
for the meaning of the gospel. We saw that "the gospel" itself
has meaning only as we recognize that it always comes out of
one particular cultural setting and enters into the new setting of
those who hear it. We saw that the gospel has been interpreted in
scores of different cultural settings during the past two millennia,
and that it exists in many different cultural settings throughout
the world today.

The question then became: what does our own culture say
today about meaning? To answer this, we looked at ways different communication technologies — oral, written, print, and electronic — have shaped cultures in the past, then how our media
culture, conforming to the demands of the capitalist spirit, has
been shaped in our time. Finally, we summarized the secular culture's worldview and the Christian worldview — and saw that
they are in fundamental conflict.

What can an ordinary Christian hope to do about this conflict? It is important to remind ourselves that such a struggle is
nothing new to the Christian. Christians have *always* found themselves to be in conflict with the secular culture in which they live.
Every generation has had to work out a response that is true to
the gospel rather than to the demands of the secular world —
faithfulness to God rather than to mammon.

The task of the second half of this book, therefore, is to examine specific problems today regarding the gospel, culture, and media in the United States and Canada. (While there are some differences, more than 70 percent of Canadians regularly watch "American TV" during the prime time hours, and the media environments in the two nations are essentially the same.[5]) After looking at some of the problems, we will then suggest positive actions Christians can take about those problems — creatively and in faith.

6

How to Read Television

> "Gracie, what was the film about?"
> "It was about two hours."
> —old George Burns–Gracie Allen exchange

> What we normally see, hear, and talk about in relation to
> a program (i.e., the story) is only about 5 percent of what
> takes place. The underlying behavior (i.e., the nonacted be-
> havior) occupies 95 percent of the program. A horse walking
> on "Bonanza" is not acting; it is the real behavior of the
> horse.
> —Tony Schwartz, media producer, 1974[1]

J. T. Pace, a sixty-three-year-old son of a former sharecropper from
Mauldin, South Carolina, will never forget the day he met the
wife of the vice-president of the United States.

In late June of 1988, Pace travelled to St. Louis to appear at
the climax of an ABC-TV three-hour special celebrating the Fourth
of July, the Bicentennial of the U.S. Constitution, and literacy. A
year before, Pace had been illiterate. He had spent much of his
life in "deception," as he called it, because of his shame and frustration. For most of his life he had used his energies to hide the
fact that he could neither read nor write.

A deeply religious man, Pace listened for hours to tapes of the
Bible. But he wanted to read it himself. So at the age of sixty-
two, he entered literacy training, and a year later he could read —
freed, as he put it, from a life of slavery.

61

Now he was to meet Barbara Bush, a strong advocate of literacy, and be introduced by her as he read the Preamble to the Constitution on national television. But there was one problem: some of the words still bothered him. He could read at eighth-grade level, but experts say it takes an eleventh-grade education to read and understand the Constitution. In particular, the word "tranquillity" bothered him; he couldn't pronounce it and didn't know what it meant. J. T. and Barbara Bush met and talked. He explained his reluctance to read the Preamble. Finally she took his hand and asked, "What if you and I read the Preamble together? J. T.'s face lit up. "I'd like that," he replied.

That evening they stood together at the podium and slowly began to read the Preamble. J. T. stumbled at some of the difficult words, but then gained confidence. Gradually Barbara Bush's voice subsided and J. T. finished reading in a strong, clear voice: "... and secure the Blessings of Liberty to ourselves and our Posterity, do ordain and establish this Constitution of the United States of America."[2]

Why is illiteracy so terrible? Because it renders a person defenseless. If you can't read, you can't tell when you are being "taken." You become an easy target for the manipulator, the trickster, the operator. Warning signs mean very little (except for their shape and color). Explanations on medicine bottles are ignored. The threat of a cut-off of your telephone is missed. You become a kind of walking invalid, unable to compete or even function in your own world.

But today even those who *can* read may be "illiterate." Today the visual image, particularly television, is replacing the printed word as the primary source of information, and very few people know how to "read" visual media like television. Fortunately, most — including the print illiterate — sense at least some of the TV's grammar. For example, when the camera moves in for a facial close-up while the music gets stronger, we expect a break — usually for a commercial. When we see a commentator's eyes moving back and forth as he speaks, we understand that he is reading a script rather than actually "talking" to us. When we hear laughter during a sit-com, we know that it is canned, not real. This intuitive understanding of the language of TV is shared by people whether they can read print or not — and therefore brings about a kind of levelling between those who can read print and those who cannot.

But almost everyone needs to learn how to read TV at an "eleventh-grade" level. For TV illiteracy has the same consequences as print illiteracy: it leaves people defenseless against the dangers of manipulation, misinformation, and propaganda.

Arthur Asa Berger, a professor of communication, suggests three ways to analyze the meaning of TV: TV as signs and symbols; TV as economics: and TV as psychology.[3] Let us look at "how to read TV" from each of these perspectives.

Reading TV as Signs and Symbols

A sign is something that stands for something else. The shape "A" stands for the first letter in our alphabet, and it stands for the sound "aee" or perhaps "ah." The shape "A" doesn't *look* like the sound "aee." Someone, far back in our history, simply attached the shape "A" to the sound "aee." In the same way, all letters, words, and most importantly, visual images of many kinds, are signs — each one signifying some concept that we have learned to associate with it.

This association between signs and concepts is the basis for TV commercials that urge us to buy something that "signifies" something else — mouthwash that signifies sweet breath and popularity, automobiles that signify power.

A symbol is somewhat different: it stands for something that is related to the symbol itself. A symbol actually *looks* like or naturally associates with what it refers to. For example, a pair of scales as the symbol of justice could not be replaced by just any other image, such as a wheel or a horse. Some symbols are very powerful, such as the American flag, the Canadian Maple Leaf, a red cross. Symbols often have strong emotional appeal.

We recognize both signs and symbols because we have learned to carry around in our heads various "codes" that help us deal with them. The codes for written words are contained in spelling and grammar — the rules by which we use such signs as "A," "B" and "C." We also have learned complicated codes of association. For example, when we hear that "he is as sharp as a tack," or that "she is as bright as a penny," we understand these as coded messages rather than as the literal truth. We have learned to decode them.

We have learned nonverbal codes as well. People are "speaking" all the time, even when they are not talking. Their dress, hair, facial expression, how they use their hands and "body language" — all tell us something about them, because we have learned how to read these visual "codes." Richard Nixon learned the importance of nonverbal codes during his famous TV debate with John F. Kennedy. The perspiration on his forehead, his dark jowls, and his tense manner were decoded by many viewers to signify someone who was not to be trusted.

Cultures are in fact systems of codes that play a crucial — and often unperceived — role in our lives. A friend of mine from Argentina once told me that, as a little boy, his German grandfather would say to him, "Before you were born, everything was already here." Gradually, as he grew older, he understood what his grandfather was trying to tell him: that the rules, the codes, the culture preceded him, and he could do very little about that. To become socialized, to be grown up, to be acculturated, means that we have learned enough of the codes of our own culture so that we can function as do other adults in our world.

The codes we are able to "read" relate fairly specifically to our own geographical location, our ethnic group, and our class. For example, every time I visit England I have to put myself on guard, because when I cross a street in the U.S. I automatically look first to my *left*, since that is where the traffic will come from. In London this code doesn't work. In fact, it can get you killed, because the traffic usually comes from the *right*. Fortunately, these days so many people from outside England visit London that most street corners have the warning: "Look Right!"

Signs, symbols and codes are one way we can read television. We can look at what we see on TV, not from the point of view of who characters are, or even what they do, but what they *mean*.

For example, consider "MASH," the eleven-year TV hit of the seventies, from the perspective of signs and symbols. What did the characters "mean"? Hawkeye, the cynical but loving doctor in perpetual search of both nurses and his own home-brewed alcohol, symbolized the frustration and immorality of war (though "MASH" was "about" the Korean War, it appeared during the Vietnam War, and some analysts believe it helped develop a national antipathy toward deeper U.S. involvement in Vietnam.) B.J., the other lead doctor, married and compassionate, represented the way all of us would like to be perceived: bright and witty but kind and understanding. Hawkeye and B.J. together "meant" authority, that doctors were in charge, not only in the operating room but in their entire tiny universe. Radar, true to his name, meant that brains and a little technology (the phones, the public address, the files) are potent problem-solvers. Margaret, the head nurse, meant that women perpetually are shortchanged in our society — misunderstood, made into clowns, yet truly competent and necessary. Father Mulcahy, the priest, meant that religion is basically peripheral to life, sometimes used for comic relief, but, when the chips are down, helpful in facing the mysteries of death.

Perhaps you agree with these interpretations of the "meaning" of the central characters of "MASH." Perhaps you don't. The point here is to realize that television can be read in terms of its signs and symbols.

We can read TV's visuals as well as its characters. Here are a few standard camera shots and editing techniques and what they "mean":

Visual	*Meaning*
Close-up	Intimacy
Medium shot	Personal relationship
Long shot	Context, setting
Angle down	Power, authority
Angle up	Weakness, smallness
Zoom in	Observation, focus
Fade in	Beginning
Fade out	Ending

In addition, as Christians, we bring our own "codes" to television. In the "MASH" program, for example, we observe that Hawkeye, in addition to being a compassionate and skilled surgeon, was also a philanderer who sought casual sex with the nurses. The doctors engaged in heavy drinking that sometimes impaired their ability to function. Men ran the show, and women were clearly secondary. Our codes as Christians pick up these meanings, and it is important that we retain this Christian perspective in an essentially secular world.

Both codes, religious and secular, are important. To understand the difference is part of what the Bible means by learning how to be in the world but not of it (1 John 2:16). We need to resist those values and meanings in our national culture that are at variance with the values and meanings which are a part of our own Christian communities. At the same time, our distinctly Christian codes of personal ethics do not reveal the *only* meanings in "MASH," and, as Christians, we also have to be sensitive and aware of the wider cultural meanings in the programs, meanings that may or may not also be Christian — the antiwar message, the compassion, the community, the healing, and, of course, the humor — and celebrate, criticize, and enjoy them as well.

Studying television as signs and symbols can be entertaining and very revealing. Decoding TV's codes can uncover some interesting hidden meanings. But constant decoding can also spoil the overall effect and power of a presentation. It's a little like evaluating a meal by analyzing each ingredient — intellectually interesting, but not totally satisfying. And this leads us to a second way of reading TV.

Reading TV as Economics

It is not generally known that Karl Marx supported himself for more than ten years by writing for a New York newspaper. Just before and during the Civil War, Marx was employed by Horace Greeley, the famous editor of the *New York World*, as that paper's European correspondent. So while Marx, writing away at the British Museum, was primarily concerned about economic theory, he also was interested in the relationship between the information people had and the ways they thought and acted.

Marx insisted that everything in a society ultimately is shaped by the economic system of that society. This includes people's ideas: "It is not the consciousness of men that determines their being, but, on the contrary, their social being determines their consciousness."[4]

In a capitalist nation such as the United States or Canada, those who benefit most from the social arrangements are the wealthy. From this perspective, the aim of the poor is to become wealthy, and the aim of the wealthy is to maintain their wealth, which means to maintain the status quo and their position in it. One way the powerful maintain the status quo is by exercising control over the ideas and information that people receive. Again, to quote Marx:

The ideas of the ruling class are, in every age, the ruling ideas: i.e., the class which is the dominant *material* force in society is at the same time its dominant *intellectual* force. The class which has the means of material production at its disposal, has control at the same time over the means of mental production.... "[5]

According to this analysis of society, those in the ruling class develop and maintain information and ideas that justify their status, and they do it in ways that make it difficult for ordinary people to recognize that they are being exploited and victimized.

Twenty-five years ago the German media analyst Hans Magnus Enzenberger made the point that all media are manipulated in some way: "There is no such thing as unmanipulated writing, filming or broadcasting. The question is therefore not whether the media are manipulated, but who manipulates them."[6]

This same critique can be used in regard to socialist and communist countries equally as well as to capitalist countries. In fact, often it is easier to see how the media are controlled, for example, in the Soviet Union or in China, because in those nations what can and cannot be printed and broadcast is governed by precise regulations, and strong, highly visible governmental agencies actively enforce those regulations. In capitalist nations the controls tend to be far more subtle. But controls are there nevertheless, as anyone who has ever attempted to influence a program or get on the air can attest.

What are the objectives of the ruling class in North America so far as the media are concerned? One is to convince people that there are no classes, and certainly no "ruling class." In the United States and Canada we live with the myth of the "classless society." There is no aristocracy, and everyone is soon on a first-name basis. But while both nations have a very large middle class, both also have a strong, and increasingly rich, upper class. At the same time both are witnessing the growth of a lower class that grows larger and poorer every year. Thus, while Marx's predictions of revolution and the permanent rule of the workers have proved to be quite inaccurate, his economic analysis can be instructive and helpful to our reading of what television really means in our society.

From the economic perspective, whenever we analyze television programming we must always ask one simple question: *who benefits*? The following questions apply to both the United States and Canada:

- Who benefits when more ads are run on television each year?

- Who benefits when the nightly news contains less and less information, and more and more entertainment?

- Who benefits when the number of documentaries on network TV decreases each year?

- Who benefits when sponsors no longer are identified with (and are thus accountable for) a particular program, but can spread their ads across many different programs (and thus have no accountability)?

- Who benefits when a single company can own television and radio stations, cable systems and local newspapers — and thus control much of the information in a whole community?

And there are some questions that apply more specifically to the United States alone:

- Who benefits when every candidate for Congress must pay thousands of dollars to local broadcasters in order to run for office?

- Who benefits when there is not a single quality series for children, Monday through Friday, on network TV?

- Who benefits because the U.S. is the only major nation in the world that actually allows commercials on programs aimed at children?

- Who benefits when the agency assigned by Congress to regulate television in the public interest instead regulates it in the interest of the broadcasters?

This is one way to "read" television — to ask who benefits by particular kinds of programs and commercials, by what is present on or absent from the screen, by the arrangements in the social system itself regarding television.

Also, we must ask: *who is injured?* Who is misled, misinformed, and softly wooed into simple acceptance of the status quo, into accepting the way things are, into believing that things can never be changed — that the poor will continue to get poorer and the rich richer? Economic analysis can have its own Christian perspective, for the Bible clearly demonstrates that God has a particular concern for the poor, the defenseless, the hopeless — in other words, those who are injured by the status quo.

While the economic perspective offers only a partial and biased way of reading TV, it is also a powerful device for examining much of what we experience on our TV screens. But there is a third approach to reading TV.

Reading TV as Psychology

Television is a factory of dreams. It reaches us at a level far below — or beyond — the level of mere thinking. Psychologists have begun to recognize the similarity of the moving image, in both film and TV, to dreaming. Dreams are visual, like a moving picture. Dreams involve us emotionally, much as a powerful story does on the large or small screen. Dreams seem to bypass our usual ways of knowing — seeing, feeling, thinking — and television and film appear to follow the same route.

We have long realized that people do not simply behave rationally. Emotions, both recognized and unexamined, also affect our behavior. A whole new field, motivation psychology, has developed to explore what causes people to think and act the ways they do. One of its founders, Ernest Dichter, tried to discover the real reasons that people do things, so that manufacturers could better shape people's behavior toward buying their products. In 1960 Dichter wrote in his book, *The Strategy of Desire:*

> Whatever your attitude toward modern psychology or psychoanalysis, it has been proved beyond any doubt that many of our daily decisions are governed by motivations over which we have no control and of which we are often quite unaware.[7]

For example, says Dichter, the unconscious reason people use cigarette lighters is that doing so gives them a sense of mastery and power — an identification that goes back to the earliest days of human experience in controlling fire. A desire for mastery and power also motivates people to drive powerful cars, to fly in powerful planes (especially corporate jets, which they "control" more directly), to carry impressive brief cases (a symbol of social power), and to engage in "power" breakfasts. It is even one reason why they seek power mowers that start — every time.

Motivation psychology asks what "uses and gratifications" the media provide. This question provides another valuable tool in helping us read TV. Instead of asking "what do the characters mean?" or "who benefits?" we ask: *what are the uses and gratifications of TV? Why does it appeal to me? What are the deeper, more basic appeals behind the surface?*

The people who plan television programming are very astute at discovering what people need, then fashioning their appeals (in both programs and ads) to meet those needs. Arthur Asa Berger identifies some twenty-one of these needs, which may also be thought of as uses or gratifications or desires:

1. To be amused.

2. To see authority figures — sometimes exalted, sometimes deflated.

3. To experience the beautiful.

4. To have shared experiences with others (community).

5. To satisfy curiosity.

6. To identify with the deity and the divine plan.

7. To find distraction and diversion.

8. To experience empathy.

9. To experience extreme emotions, such as love and hate, the horrible and terrible — but in a guilt-free and controlled situation.

10. To find models to imitate.

11. To gain an identity.

12. To gain information about the world.

13. To reinforce our belief in justice.

14. To believe in romantic love.

15. To believe in magic, the marvelous, the miraculous.

16. To see others make mistakes.

17. To participate in history (vicariously, without risk).

18. To be purged of unpleasant emotions.

19. To obtain outlets for our sexual drives in a guilt-free context.

20. To explore taboo subjects safely.

21. To affirm moral, spiritual, and cultural values.[8]

This is a good check list for reading television's psychological appeal. Of course, once we become conscious of the appeal of a particular program or character or action, then we can ask whether that appeal is important or trivial, valid or invalid, humanizing or dehumanizing, Christian or non-Christian. In other words, we can *deal* with it. And when we learn how to deal with television, it loses much of its power over us.

Television continually tries to convince us that we have complete "freedom," while at the same time creating in us anxieties and dissatisfactions that can be resolved only by buying something, by believing something, or by doing something that television suggests. This is why TV is so appealing and at the same time so frustrating. This is also why it is so dangerous: it has the potential to dominate us while making us think we are acting in perfect freedom.

And this is why the experience of J. T. Pace and other illiterates is important. Their experience of print illiteracy simply illustrates in a vivid way the effect that *media* illiteracy is having on all of us. J. T. found that reading print freed him from a life of "virtual slavery." But everyone, using the various techniques of analysis I have described in this chapter, can learn to read television — and that will help to free us, too.

7

How the Church Uses Television

> Again, the devil took Jesus to a very high mountain, and
> showed him all the kingdoms of the world and the glory
> of them; and he said to him, "All these I will give you, if
> you will fall down and worship me." Then Jesus said to him,
> "Begone, Satan! for it is written, 'You shall worship the Lord
> your God, and him only shall you serve.'"
>
> –Matthew 4:8–10

H. L. Menken, a political commentator during the 1930s, said that
for every difficult and complicated question, there is an answer
that is simple, easily understood ... and *wrong*.

It is not easy for churches to deal with the task of communicating their message in today's culture. Never before in history have
the audiences been so vast, the religious differences so great, the
technology so powerful. Yet many Christians insist on responses
that are simple, easily understood, and often quite wrong in terms
of good theology, good communication, and plain common sense.

One highly visible attempt to communicate the gospel today
is the Electronic Church. Actually, religious broadcasting in the
United States and Canada is far more extensive than the Electronic Church. In the U.S. some two dozen "mainline" national
denominations — such as the United Methodist Church and the
Episcopal Church as well as the Roman Catholic Church — provide programs ranging from thirty-second spots to half-hour programs fifty-two weeks a year. Protestant, Catholic, and Jewish national organizations produce programs aired regularly on the three
commercial TV networks. More than thirty "evangelical" or con-

servative religious groups, definitely not a part of the Electronic Church — Seventh-Day Adventists, Southern Baptists, Missouri Synod Lutherans, and others — provide programs on hundreds of TV stations. Hundreds of local religious programs, produced by local churches, are carried without charge by local stations, and Councils of Churches in some cities have paid staff who place religious discussion and news programs on local TV and radio stations. In 1989 several Christian denominations cooperated in developing VISN, a religious cable service fed by satellite. By the end of 1989, VISN was available to approximately six million cable homes in the U.S., and the programming provided by the member groups was supplied for eighteen hours daily.

In Canada the Protestant and Roman Catholic churches have cooperated for many years with the CBC in producing programs seen nationwide on its network. Also, hundreds of local churches have services aired on local radio and TV stations. In addition, several Christian evangelists have purchased time for both local and national programming. On September 1, 1988, VISION-TV, a multifaith national television service became available on the basic cable system to almost five million Canadian homes. VISION-TV broadcasts a variety of drama, documentary, music, and public affairs programming in addition to religious programs. The service is supported almost entirely by the faith groups in Canada thus far, but it is negotiating for a per-subscriber fee from cable companies. The major faith groups involved are identified as Baha'i, Buddhist, Christian, Hindu, Muslim, Jewish, Native Spirituality, Sikh, Unitarian, and Zoroastrian.

So the Electronic Church is only one part of a large religious broadcasting effort going on in the United States and Canada. By "Electronic Church," I mean specifically those programs: that are nationally distributed through purchased time; that depend on a single highly visible charismatic leader (Pat Robertson, Oral Roberts, Robert Schuller); that exhibit high-budget, "slick" production qualities; that consistently solicit money over the air; and that make extensive use of telephone campaigns and computerized "personal" letters to contact viewers.

Surprisingly, when one thinks of the mass audiences attracted to TV, the audience for the Electronic Church is not large. It has not been growing in the last decade. In the U.S., the A. C. Nielsen ratings report that the number of viewers for Electronic Church programs probably peaked around 1978 and has been holding steady or even decreasing ever since. In 1984, an Annenberg-Gallup study revealed that the total number of viewers who watch one hour or more of religious programs per week is about 4.84 million persons, or 2.17 percent of the total population. Most of the Electronic Church programming aired in Canada is imported from the U.S., and while the aggregate audience for their programs is proportionately small, Canadian donations in response to appeals from these U.S.-based groups is sufficiently large to justify many of them having specific Canadian post office addresses.

Nevertheless, the Electronic Church has made a significant impact on American society. It has changed the perception of what many consider to be "religion." It has had significant social and political impact, particularly in the early 1980s, bringing into visibility a religious subgroup not previously taken seriously either by the mainline churches or by the society at large. And it has challenged the mainline churches to rethink their own relationship with the mass media.

Reading the Electronic Church as Sign and Symbol

In Chapter 6 we described three techniques that we can use to "read" television. Of course, these techniques apply to *all* kinds of TV — news, sitcoms, commercials, and every other format. But in order to test them in a real-life situation, let us apply the techniques to the Electronic Church. In so doing we will have a "test run" of ways to analyze all TV programs, and at the same time we will gain a better understanding of the Electronic Church.

First we ask: what do the various signs and symbols *mean?* For several years I have been leading discussion groups that look at clips of several of the top televangelists, then list the signs and symbols. Some images most often mentioned, with suggestions about their meanings, are:

Sign, symbol	Meaning
Robe, preacher center of attention	Authority: in the person
Pulpit, reference to Bible	Authority: in the book
Reference to charts, diagrams	Authority: in the "answers"
Speaking to huge rallies	Authority: in large numbers
Interviews with celebrities	Importance of worldly success
Interviews with business*men*	Importance of wealth (sexism)
Banks of phone-answers	"Personalizes" call-ins
Wearing expensive clothes	Person is a success, role model
Country-western music	Religion can be fun

Dramatic "pulpit-thumping"   Appeal to emotions, entertainment
Give-aways (books, objects)   Attempt to tie viewer to program
Sale of books, objects   Similarity to commercial TV

One has only to view a program or two to discover that many
visual messages hide behind the verbal messages on TV. It can
be enlightening to analyze the televangelists from the perspective
of their program's signs and symbols — as it can be for all TV
programs.

Reading the Electronic Church as Economics

Second, we ask: who benefits? Who profits from the particular
program, appeal, or message? Is the program designed to meet
the needs and interests of various viewers, of those who seek
religious inspiration, or new insights into the Bible, or strength
to meet the problems of their lives? An economic analysis reveals some of the most often-expressed criticisms of the Electronic
Church. The scandals surrounding a number of the televangelists have revealed that some are taking a great deal of money
from people and using it for their own benefit. For example, in
1987 a class action suit was filed against Jim and Tammy Bakker
on behalf of some 161,000 donors to the Bakker's PTL programs
who had paid $1,000 each to become "lifetime partners," a sta-
tus which included free accommodations at the PTL theme park.[1]
Only one of the promised motel-like units was built, and there
never was enough room for participants. The suit charged that
the Bakkers and their top aides had diverted millions of dollars
to their personal use. Jim Bakker was convicted and sentenced to
forty-five years in prison.

Another criticism is that televangelists have used too much of
donor income merely to raise more money. For example, in 1982
Jimmy Swaggart spent $38 million — more than 80 percent of his
total income — just keeping his program on the air.[2] And in 1982
Jerry Falwell spent $5 in fund-raising for every $7 he raised.[3]

An interesting comparison of "who benefits" was made by
Norman Dewire, of the United Methodist Church General Council on Ministries, who pointed out that "the national United
Methodist Church runs on *five cents of each $1*, and with the rest
supports 750 missionaries, 900 short-term missionaries, curriculum and worship materials, the largest network of private colleges in the United States, one hundred retirement homes, and

the recruitment and training of ministers plus all communication materials."[4]

Even more serious is the aspect that appears when we ask the corollary question: who is injured? An article in *Harpers* described one of the CBN "700 Club" on-air fund raising events, during which Ben Kinchlow, Pat Robertson's aide, rushed up to the microphone and said to Pat:

"We have a report just in from Charlottesville, Virginia," Ben said. "A lady with an ingrown toenail sent in $100 along with her Seven Lifetime Prayer Requests. Within a week — get this — *three* of those *lifetime* prayer requests have been answered!"

"Praise *God!*" Pat said. "And that's not all," said Ben. "The toenail was miraculously healed the *very next day!*"

"Praise God! Robertson said. "You know, you can't out-give God."

Some time later in the program, Ben once again comes on screen:

"Pat, here is a report from a woman in California," Kinchlow said, dashing up with a message just taken by one of the phone counselors. "She's on a limited income, and with all sorts of health problems, too. She decided to trust in God and to step out in faith on the Kingdom Principles. She was already giving half her disability money to the 700 Club to spread the gospel of Jesus Christ. But just last week, she decided to go *all the way*, and to give God the money she spends for cancer medicine — $120 a month. And three days later — get this! — from an entirely unexpected source, she got a check for *three thousand dollars!*"

"Praise *God!* Robertson said. *"Let's give God a hand!"*

Clearly the woman who gave all her cancer-treatment money to this ministry was injuring herself. But what about the other woman, the one who had three of her "Lifetime Prayer Requests" answered in one week — plus her ingrown toenail healed? Was she sustaining any injury by being encouraged to partake in a trivialization of prayer and the meaning of religion? If people can truly have half of their "lifetime" prayer requests answered in one week, then perhaps all our churches can go out of business.

When we look at the Electronic Church programs and ask who benefits and who is injured, the answers are not encouraging.

Reading the Electronic Church as Psychology

And third, we ask: what uses and gratifications are met by the Electronic Church?

In Chapter 6 we listed more than a score of uses and gratifications that people seem to seek from TV. This list names *needs* that people bring not only to TV but to all of life. Psychologists say that people have genuine needs to be amused, to experience the beautiful, to experience extreme emotions, to satisfy their curiosity, and so on. Which of these are met by the Electronic Church?

In one way or another, just about all of them. Not only do televangelists appeal to people's need to identify with the deity and the divine plan, but they skillfully identify and appeal to almost every need on the list. Let us take a more or less random half of these needs and suggest the appeal a televangelist might make in meeting them.

Need	*Appeal*
To be amused	Jimmy Swaggart's music and humor
To see authority exalted	Jerry Falwell's TV skills; Pat Robertson's bid for the U.S. presidency
To see authority deflated	Bakker and Swaggart scandals
To experience beauty	"Hour of Power" music
To share experience with others	Joining the "700 Club" or "PTL Club," becoming a "Prayer Partner"
To identify with the divine plan	Robertson's charts, Falwell's and Oral Roberts's prooftexts
To experience empathy	Robertson's and Bakker's talks with guests — "just plain folks"
To experience extreme emotions: love/hate	Swaggart's attacks on liberals, Catholics
To find models to imitate	Falwell's certainty; Robertson's suavity
To gain information	Robertson's explanations of world events
To believe in magic	Healing claims tied to donations

Although needs are abbreviated and the "appeals" mere suggestions, the chart shows that we can learn a great deal about television — any television — by analyzing the uses people put it to, and the gratifications they get from it.

Pros and Cons

Granted that the needs people bring to the televangelists are genuine, the question then becomes: *how* do the televangelists meet
them? Are their responses helpful and positive, with the viewers'
good uppermost, or do they manipulate people for other purposes?

A simple yes or no is not possible. Televangelists differ greatly
in their motivations, their techniques, their messages and approaches. And an audience of several million is bound to produce
many different levels of response to the same program, because
what people bring to the programs differs, and consequently, the
programs' effects on them will differ.

Stewart M. Hoover, a professor of communication, wrote a
book on the effects of the Electronic Church. As a graduate stu-
dent, Hoover participated in the Annenberg-Gallup study of the
Electronic Church. Later he focused on one program, the "700
Club," conducting extensive interviews with twenty individuals
or couples that the study identified as heavy viewers.[5] He lists
a number of ways in which viewing the "700 Club" appears to
satisfy the needs of these viewers. His list recalls many of the
"uses and gratifications" mentioned above:

> For most viewers, the "700 Club" serves many of the classic
> "functions" of mass media. It provides news and informa-
> tion. It orients them to the wider range of activities and in-
> volvements of the evangelical parachurch. It introduces them
> to other evangelicals, fundamentalists, or charismatics with
> whom they can identify, and from whom they can learn.
> It provides entertainment in the form of music and "good
> preaching."[6]

Hoover found that the most religiously useful function of the
"700 Club" was that it was *available*, in viewers' homes, on a day-
to-day basis, so that when crisis or difficulty occurred, it could
"be there for them."[7] Hoover also found that viewers felt that
through watching the "700 Club" they were recovering "the authentic religious faith of their individual and cultural roots," because for them the program expressed conservative or fundamen-
talist Christianity. Interestingly, for them it represented a "higher
stage of evangelicalism," because it was able to give expression to
their views in a national, public way (through television) which

had not been possible with older forms of conservatism and fundamentalism.[8]

The very fact that "their" program was "on TV" gave it great prestige and indicated its success. Says Hoover, "By appearing on and being part of television (secular modernism at its most profane), the '700 Club' transcends the lower-class origins of the evangelicalism and fundamentalism out of which it springs."[9]

This appeal, however, has a drawback, for Hoover found that the program itself merely reinforced what viewers already believed, and that they supported it not so much because it helped *them* but because they thought it would be good for *others*:

> The program is seen simply as consistent with their religious consciousness, but it is valuable to them for its divergence from the traditional evangelical or fundamentalist worldview. For all of them, the program's appeal to a broader, outside world in terms of class and theology is its major attraction. It deserves support not so much because *they themselves* are the objects of its ministries, but because of what it does for, and represents to, the rest of the world. With few exceptions, these viewers see the "700 Club" as there for "someone else."[10]

This rationale, of course, strikes at the heart of all televangelists' appeal for funds: to reach the unreached. Hoover's analysis concludes that "... the electronic church holds out promise mainly for those who are most easily convinced, not for a broader society in need of some sort of help."

The Electronic Church surely meets the needs of some people. An aggregate of several millions will include some people whose needs are being met in adequate and genuine ways. On balance, however, the Electronic Church has tended to mislead people and to provide them with a message that has very little relationship to the gospel of Jesus Christ which they claim to serve.

The fundamental problem is that in order to reach the audiences necessary in order to raise large sums of money, the televangelists compromised the gospel until it had very little resemblance to the gospel. James Brieg expressed it this way:

> The programs are a distortion of the gospel. There is no cross. In a half-hour, they have to convert you (which trivi-

alizes what conversion means), heal you (which is hokey), promise success (people on the shows have overcome alcoholism, are Miss America, or play in the NFL), and entertain (so they find ever more expensive sets with more fountains and glamour which detract from the world of the suffering).[11]

In summary, the Electronic Church aspect of religious television today is driven primarily by considerations of economics and power. Expecting to use the enormous power of television for their own purposes, the televangelists have instead been used by it. They have had to conform their messages to meet the demands of TV — demands to get larger audiences to get more money to get more stations to get even larger audiences. In order to get larger audiences, their messages had to please the audience, and never offend them, a requirement that becomes fatal to any authentic proclamation of the Christian faith.

It is an open question whether some televangelists were corrupted by the power of the media or simply found in the media a comfortable fit for their kind of religious evangelism. Undoubtedly both factors have been at work. Most evangelists have bought into the world of commercial television to reap its rewards of vast audience reach; in many cases they stayed to benefit from its rewards of money, power, and prestige. They used one of the most powerful institutions in our culture, and, inevitably, that power began to corrupt them. The scandals of Oral Roberts, Jim and Tammy Bakker, and Jimmy Swaggart are only the surface manifestations of this corruption; far more serious are programs that denigrate authentic Christianity in the name of Christianity and make use of God in the name of God, misleading millions of persons about the nature of genuine religious experience.

How TV Should Be Used by the Churches

How should the churches respond to the challenge presented by the Electronic Church, and to the even more fundamental challenge of how to communicate the Christian faith in a media culture? What should the churches be doing to "use" television in ways faithful to the gospel?

The churches must continue to work in the area of programming. The existence of dangers should not deter churches from the enormous potential for good that television represents. But the solution does not lie in the directions taken by the Electronic Church.

When mainline churches seek to use broadcasting to examine biblical Christianity in relation to society today, they run up against great moral ambiguity. Transcendent religious values are so much at odds with society's values that it is difficult and often impossible to deal seriously with significant issues on radio and television. It is possible, of course, to find ways to use mass media to sensitize people to moral and spiritual values. But the dangers of being taken in by the media are so subtle and so powerful that religious communicators need to approach all programming in television and radio with the greatest caution and theological sensitivity.

I believe that the church should use radio and TV for *pre-evangelism*. On one hand, the church cannot *be* the church on radio and television. It cannot "broadcast" genuine community, or provide the baptisms, marriages, and funerals, the celebrations and confessions that a worshipping church provides. Broadcasting cannot be the place for personal confessions, because it does not establish direct contact between speaker and the listener-viewers. Technology changes the nature of communication, and a worship service "broadcast" is simply not the same thing as a worship service in which one participates personally. I doubt that serious religious questions can be answered satisfactorily and in depth on radio and television. But on the other hand, we can give information about the Christian faith, and *the right questions can be raised*. People can be helped to ask who they are and what they are here for and whether they have any worth, and if so, why.

Unfortunately, the church has tended to fall into the trap of the technology mythmakers and ask what works and how to get results, rather than what is true and how to increase insights and perceptions that lead to the truth. The church can use the mass media but as *preparation for the gospel* rather than as "mediation" of the gospel, because the gospel, to be true, requires the presence of persons, not machines.

Using media to prepare people to receive the gospel involves three steps. First, it requires exploring with people what theologian Paul Tillich called the "boundary situations," those points at which modern men and women reach the limits of their human existence, where they sense a lack of personal meaning or fear being useless and worthless. Second, it requires affirming through the media persons and events that have been able to deal with these "boundary situations" creatively and with faith: news stories from Manila and South Africa; biographies of Gandhi, Martin Luther King, Mother Teresa, Archbishop Tutu — and a host of other unfamous people of faith as well. And third, it requires pointing to the churches as the place where people can go to begin to work out their salvation, find community, and discover the power of confession and forgiveness.

Canadian VISION-TV offers a good example. Rita Deverell, host of "It's About Time," which airs daily on the new network, says, "My show is not really about religion in any direct way. My show is about people and about their attempts to find solutions in their small ways for the serious problems of the world. In doing that, it's important...to interact with people who are on a spiritual quest." Similarly, "Catch the Spirit," a United Methodist Church series produced for the U.S. VISN cable service, documents ways Christians are meeting genuine needs in local communities and throughout the world.

Religious broadcasting can help lead people to understand what the gospel message is, and can encourage them to go where they can get more answers and possibly, to use a decidedly nonmedia term, become saved. That place is, simply, the church. Television should be a signpost, *a servant of the local church — and never the other way around.*

TV, as well as all mass media, must be used as a tool, but used very critically, constantly striving not to succumb to the temptations of the power that the media tend to confer, not to allow church leaders to become media celebrities or programs to become so caught up in the demands of media that the gospel ceases to be the gospel at all.

8

Television News: Who's in Control?

A free press is the triumph of humanity over oppression.
                                                    –Thomas Jefferson[1]

From TV's beginning, news was considered one of its greatest strengths. The idea that events occurring hundreds or even thousands of miles away can be brought directly into the home has enormous appeal. When a coast-to-coast hook-up was achieved, millions of viewers were amazed to see the sun setting over the towers of New York City, and, in the next moment, the same sun, high in the sky, shining down on San Francisco's Golden Gate Bridge. It was not long before the TV signal was able to leap the ocean. The coronation of Queen Elizabeth II in June 1953 was one of the first events seen by a worldwide audience. And what adult can forget Monday, July 20, 1969, at 10:56 a.m. Eastern Standard Time, the moment when Neil Armstrong placed the first human footprint on the moon — "one giant leap for mankind!" — live, on TV.

We somehow feel that what we can see with our own eyes is *true*, even when what we are seeing is mediated through the lens of a camera, thousands of transistors, miles of wire, and millions of phosphors projected on the back of a picture tube.

But the raw elements of news — the disasters, riots, hearings, and interviews — are only rarely allowed to come into our living rooms unedited and unplanned. Instead, "news," particularly on television, is carefully filtered, edited, and choreographed to fit a pattern — a pattern that meets both the need of society to have its basic cultural worldview reinforced, and even more important, the need of the communication industry to reach and hold the largest possible audience. And, as we shall see, that industry is both growing and centralizing very rapidly.

Media Monopoly

Alexis de Tocqueville, when visiting the United States in 1831, remarked that since the American press has "established no central control over the expression of opinion," therefore "nothing is easier than to set up a newspaper, and a small number of readers suffices to defray the expenses of the editors."[2]

Today, few things are more difficult than to set up a metropolitan newspaper. In fact, the number daily papers has been decreasing for more than fifty years. In 1900 in the USA there were 2,042 daily papers and 2,034 owners. By 1980 there were 1,730 dailies and 760 owners. In 1900 there was, on average, one newspaper owner for every 38,000 citizens. By 1980 the average newspaper owner provided the news for 300,000 citizens.[3] Thus while media concentration increases, the diversity of views decreases.

In 1920 there were 700 cities in the United States with at least two competing dailies, whereas in 1983, with the population more than doubled, only 27 cities had more than one daily paper.[4] Competing newspapers continue to go out of business. When the *Washington Star* folded in 1981, Washington, D.C., was left with only one paper, which made it unique among the capitals of major nations: London has eleven dailies, Paris fourteen, Rome eighteen, Tokyo seventeen, and Moscow nine.[5]

Diversity of views is being further strangled by the takeover of the remaining dailies by a few large chains. Of the 1,700 daily papers today in the USA, more than 1,200 have been absorbed by chains that control 80 percent of all daily newspaper circulation. In Canada, press concentration is even greater. According to a report by the Royal Commission on Newspapers in 1981, three chains control 90 percent of French-language daily circulation. In seven provinces, two-thirds or more of total newspaper circulation is controlled by a single chain.[6] And just two chains, Southam and Thomson, control about 70 percent of all daily English-language newspaper circulation.[7]

In addition, newspapers and television stations are being used by a few corporations to form super-media groups. For example, CBS is not only in television and radio, but also in magazines, books, and cable TV; Capital Cities, which owns ABC, also is in newspapers and radio. The Gannett newspaper chain shares board of directors members with Allegheny Airlines, Phillips Petroleum, Merrill Lynch, McDonnell Douglas Aircraft, Standard Oil of Ohio, McGraw-Hill, 20th Century Fox, Kellogg, and New York Telephone, among others.[8]

The interlocking of business with information industries is bound to affect content. One all too typical example is given by the relationship that existed between Cleveland's only daily newspaper and its largest bank:

> Through a trust, the bank shared control of the *Cleveland Plain Dealer*...for more than half a century. The bank's chairman was also the paper's chairman, and one minority shareholder recalls discovering that the paper "had 7 million in a checking account at the bank drawing no interest.... After the [bank's] sale [in 1967], the *Plain Dealer*'s columns began criticizing the bank. "How much the bank [had] managed the news I'm not sure," says a former staff member, "but I do know we never printed the story that [the late bank chairman George] Gund was the biggest slumlord in town."[9]

The growth of media concentration, especially the news media, continues unabated, and each year "news" becomes increasingly dominated by the interests of large corporations. Of all the threats to our freedom of information in the U.S. and Canada, the most tangible at present is the threat of economic monopoly. When the variety of sources of news and information dries up to only a few, the result can be that news is treated not so much as information as ideology.

News as Ideology

Today, in spite of its claim of "that's the way it is," TV news is already the expression of an ideology. In the U.S. this ideology tells us that the country, and indeed the whole world, is a rather simple place. This ideology sees the world in terms of good and bad, us and them, free and slave, the free West and the communist East, with very little complexity and almost no historical perspective, context, or explanations.

In the early 1980s, Bruhn Jensen at the University of Copenhagen conducted an analysis of the news on two U.S. networks,

CBS and ABC. He concluded that their news portrays society as divided into three separate spheres of activity: the private sphere, which includes the individual, family, and private enterprise; the public sphere, where "politics" and "the economy" operate; and the state sphere, where agencies of the government maintain political, economic, and social stability.[10] The central element in this system is the public sphere, which contains the press, the political parties, and the other political institutions which together operate in a democratic fashion to set the terms of cooperation between the private sector, including business, and the state. Thus, according to the news media, the public sphere (the press, public expressions, and voting) is the central location of power in our industrialized nations. But this ideology does not allow us to consider that perhaps private business decisions are in fact making some political decisions more or less inevitable, or that the media themselves may be controlled more by economic considerations than by a devotion to democratic principles of free expression.

Such a scenario is unsettling. In North America we always have thought of our press as the basic medium for the free and open discussion of ideas, the extension of the soapbox, the essential element which makes possible the shaping of public opinions and decisions. But our huge "press" today, including the electronic press, is in fact increasingly shaped by the operations of the economic marketplace. As large corporations have come to dominate almost every public expression, replacing the soapbox, the town meeting and the penny press with nationwide and even worldwide newspaper and TV coverage, the economic considerations of business tend to push aside such democratic considerations as the free interchange of information and ideas.

The news media today are structured as an integral part of the corporate economy. They are designed, first, to produce *profit* and, second, to reproduce the *status quo* — the prevailing social order. And their *news* function takes a back seat to both. Profits flow from the ability of a newspaper or television station to attract the largest possible audience, not its ability to provide the most careful and balanced news service. And support for the *status quo* merely enforces the power of those already in command and reduces the opportunity for change.

Let us see exactly how this happens. Jensen and his researchers studied a full week of the ABC and CBS nightly news broadcasts during the week of September 18–24, 1981. They focused on coverage that considered economic activity: there were forty-nine such stories that week. The researchers were particularly impressed with what was left *out* of the stories. For example, concerning the rising inflation rate, the CBS story said:

> Before March, inflation measured by consumer prices ripped along at a double-digit pace, the annual rate above 10 per cent. Then came four months below 10 per cent. In July, the inflation rate as measured by consumer prices jumped back up to an annual rate of 15.2 per cent. Today the Labor Department reported the figures for August. Consumer prices up eight-tenths of one per cent, which makes the most current annual inflation rate 10.6 per cent.

Note that CBS describes inflation as "ripping along," "jumping," and "(going) up" — almost as though it moves by itself. But the *causes* receive no consideration at all. Why is inflation going up? Why did it "rip along" and then drop? Why is it going up again? And, from the viewpoint of the citizen, what might be done about it?

When inflation is portrayed as automatic, and when no context or explanations are provided, there is little wonder that average Americans feel that inflation is a self-contained power beyond their reach and understanding, and consequently a force that transcends their ability to do anything constructive about it. The research revealed similarly that many indexes — the Dow Jones Index, the price of gold, and various others — are all are portrayed as if they have lives of their own. Thus "the economy" is presented as a force working on its own, beyond comprehension by the average person or action by the average citizen.

In another economic story dealing with a protest conducted against a California utility's nuclear power plant by a local organization, the CBS coverage said:

> It cost thousands for extra National Guardsmen, highway patrol men and sheriff's deputies. Construction was stopped for a few hours when protesters blockaded the main gate. Some nuclear scientists sympathetic to the protester's cause wonder if the demonstration did any good: "I don't expect that the protest will result in the plant not operating. I think that

the plant will operate, simply because of the pressure of the investment."

Here is another lesson in the futility of attempts by citizens to deal with economic matters. After listing the negative effects of the protest movement, the report implies that the demonstration will make no difference anyway. Even a supporter questions whether it did "any good." The quotation not only substantiates the futility of the protest but also the inevitability of the plant opening. CBS then concludes its report:

> The National Guard was never needed at the front lines. One small group did put on a lunch-time concert for those protecting the plant. (Footage of demonstrators singing) The demonstration is expected to go on, perhaps for weeks. Company officials still insist that once the plant is on line next year and producing cheap power, some who oppose it now may sing another tune.

Note that the public protest is "the front lines," implying a kind of war in which the National Guard represents "our" side — against the protesters. The National Guard helped the police whose legitimate and designated role was "protecting the plant" against the protesters (rather than seeing that both sides to the dispute have opportunity to be heard). In the closing sentence, the news report places its editorial weight with the company officials as it is assumed that the plant will be "on line next year" and that it will be "producing cheap power." The message is clear: this is a temporary disruption of the social order and when it goes away, the business of business will continue to be the most important value.

While this analysis of network news is selective and fragmentary, it does illustrate a basic problem we face as we search for meaning in our complex world. Mass media news in general, and television news in particular, oversimplify issues to the point of distortion. In addition, they represent an ideological bias that strongly supports the existing economic, social, and political powers.

In our consumption of news we depend upon a quality called journalistic "professionalism" to protect us against such distortion and misinformation. But journalists are human beings, after all, and except for a few extraordinary situations such as Watergate and Vietnam, most tend to take the course of least resistance. They are more inclined to accept explanations from official sources, from "experts," from company officials, from well prepared hand-outs created by public relations experts, than to go to the trouble to dig out opposing views that often are represented by small, inefficient, underfinanced and even unpopular groups. Thus what journalists report as "news" tends to coincide with the vision of officials, experts and companies. The journalists' vision tends to express the vision of those in power, which thus becomes their ideology, whether or not they intend it to be, even *whether or not they know it to be.*

And since the news operations are themselves part of vast conglomerations of business power, the management of these corporations, through their selection of staff, their promulgation of policy "guidelines," and their intricate and subtle system of rewards and punishments, oversee and maintain a news environment that fosters not so much facts and understanding as profit and the prevailing social order.

TV as Election Spoiler

Perhaps our most sacred secular act is voting. James Madison wrote in 1798 that "the people, not the government, possess the absolute sovereignty." He believed that the way the people expressed their political will, short of riot and revolution, was through popular elections. And today, the way people make their electoral decisions is by learning about the issues and candidates primarily through the print and electronic press.

Madison's vision of democracy depended on an informed electorate "examining public characters and measures." The voters would actively participate in the public policy debate. But recent elections have demonstrated that citizens are becoming more and more removed from the electoral process, with little chance even to *watch* a genuine debate among the candidates, much less to participate in the give and take themselves.

Robert Dahl, a respected political scientist, commented about the 1988 election process in the U.S.: "It represents a real loss of control by the electorate over the process of government. People are no longer controlling the major questions of policy that the winner will have to deal with." Dahl then zeroed in on television coverage:

Voters are asked to make judgments about the character of
the candidates — without real discussion, with advertising
and sound bites that trivialize their differences and give limited and prejudicial information. There's no other democratic
system in the world that puts so heavy a burden on its citizens in choosing the chief executive. Democracy requires
that questions be posed in an intelligible way.[11]

While newspapers certainly are not blameless, it is television
that has become the spoiler of elections in the United States. TV
has corrupted the process in at least three ways. First, commercial
TV has consistently refused to provide time as a public service to
all candidates. Thus electoral information becomes a commodity.
Instead of treating their license to broadcast as an obligation to
provide air time for all candidates so that voters may be informed,
broadcasters have turned electioneering into a huge profit-making
scheme that charges ever-greater prices to candidates who wish to
be heard. As a result, everyone loses — except the broadcasters.
And while public broadcasters are willing to provide time, U.S.
presidential candidates have shied away from appearing only on
the Public Broadcasting System.

Second, as part of its economic incentive, TV has encouraged shorter and shorter exposure of both candidates and issues.
For example, the length of the average U.S. network television
news "sound bite" (itself an insult to the voter's intelligence)
dropped from 11.8 seconds in the 1984 campaign to 9 seconds in
1988. Nine seconds of cryptic slogans — "read my lips," "no new
taxes" — is totally inadequate to explain how any candidate proposes to reduce the foreign debt and balance the budget without
increasing taxes.

Also, during the Reagan administration, TV developed the
photo-opportunity into an art, though hardly an informative one.
The photo-op is simply a triumph of pictures over ideas, and TV
producers, once again driven by economic rather than public service pressures, have allowed the pictures to dominate the copy,
and thus the image to replace substance. And everyone — even
most broadcasters — agree that the 1988 presidential candidate
"debates" were not debates at all, but a carefully scripted tip-
toe of bland questions not being answered by carefully rehearsed
candidates, a charade boring rather than enlightening the viewers.

Third, TV, and the press in general, has begun to rely on

polling as an alternative to investigative reporting — a way to deal with issues more easily and inexpensively than old-fashioned digging into the candidates' past performance. But the press has special protection because it is expected to clarify, to set in context, to suggest alternatives, to seek out informed expressions and viewpoints on all sides, in other words, to help develop Madison's informed electorate.

In 1988 each of the major U.S. television networks worked with a major newspaper — CBS News with the *New York Times*, NBC News with the *Wall Street Journal*, and ABC News with the *Washington Post* — in order to produce polls which themselves mightily influenced both politicians and public. This kind of polling results in a circular process: politicians look to polls to find out "what the public thinks," then modify their image and views to conform, while citizens eagerly consult the polls to find out what they themselves are thinking and which candidate most closely resembles the results of the polls. Consider, for example, the effect of an ABC News report, aired more than a month before the election, that featured a state-by-state poll declaring Mr. Bush the winner.

An additional misuse of polling is the networks' computerized predictions on election night. For at least the past decade, in both Canadian and U.S. federal elections, network newscasters have "announced" a winner long before millions of voters in the western parts of each nation had an opportunity to vote.

What can be done about TV's spoiler effect? Fortunately there are still workable solutions. Most crucial in the U.S. would be reversing the deregulation of radio and TV, which has encouraged broadcasters to put their own economic self-interest ahead of the public interest. Regulation is a key moral issue.* In addition, citizens, through Congress, could enact a few simple — but politically difficult — remedies:

1. Make all presidential candidates' receipt of federal election funds conditional on their willingness to participate in several unscripted, genuine face-to-face debates. Another tactic to insure real debate would be to ask candidates to confront one another on TV for three hours; after the first hour or so, candidates could no longer dodge questions or avoid revealing their real attitudes and thinking processes to the public. The 1988 election campaign

---

*This issue is discussed in more detail on pp. 125–127.

in Canada did precisely this. Two genuine debates were held on national TV, each three hours in length, one in English, one in French — both without the benefit of journalists. And it resulted in Canadians learning a great deal about their candidates' views on significant issues and their approaches to problems facing the nation.

2. Require television stations, as a condition of their license, to give a certain amount of free time to all candidates. If candidates accept, they would not be allowed to purchase additional time. Again, Canada and England have such requirements, and broadcasters provide this service and still manage to make acceptable profits, not from elections, but from advertising related to their regular entertainment programming.

3. Close all polls at the same time. One suggestion is a twenty-four-hour voting day; another would be to close the polls throughout the nation at, for example, 10 p.m. Eastern (7 p.m. Pacific time). Several such proposals are being considered by Congress.

In Canada the situation is somewhat different. Federal candidates are offered free time for debates, and so it is important that citizens at least hold the line on existing regulations of the Canadian Radio-television and Telecommunications Commission. However, the closing of polls at one time through Canada, as in the U.S., would help insure that all voters have an equal opportunity to vote before "election results" begin to be announced.

TV inherently personalizes news and public events through close-ups that allow viewers to scrutinize the faces and "style" of the men and women who appear on the screen. This means that, lacking the information necessary to determine where the truth lies, viewers must rely on relatively superficial impressions to judge whom they believe can be trusted. An issue-oriented political party, with its platform and issues, is thus easily circumvented; viewers can vote for the person whose style and charm appears most appealing. Their attention is channeled toward cues about how one "feels" about a candidate rather than to past record or position on particular issues.

Personalized politics is here to stay. There is no reasonable expectation that communication-by-personality will be eliminated. But there are ways in which we can expect the television industry itself to take into consideration this new process and to use it to benefit, rather than befuddle, us as viewers. For example, extensive interviews give a viewer a completely different feel for a candidate than does a nine-second "sound bite." Genuine debates rather than stiff, formal, and unreal appearances by candidates mouthing formula responses would add immeasurably to the voters' ability to make informed decisions. And while issue-oriented analysis by TV journalists rather than a daily "story" handed out by the campaign managers might cost a network more money, it would begin to meet the ethical norms of good journalism as well as the needs of the electorate.

Conclusions

Madison's vision of free and open communication in a democracy is not just another theory; it is basic to a democratic nation's welfare. But if the people turn over the channels of communication to commerce, then profits and not public welfare will guide who communicates and what is communicated. The Good News celebrates the worth of every person, not only the rich, and the idea that everyone — both rich and poor — should have a say in the way their lives are governed is a major implication of the gospel. Thus while Christians may differ regarding particular candidates and issues, there can be little disagreement among them that information about candidates and issues is of fundamental importance. If elections are to remain open and free, then Christians among others are going to have to insist that television, their primary source of information, meet its public service obligation and cease to be the election spoiler.

Also, by choosing to deal with some problems and ignoring others, television news shapes the public's political priorities. The research shows that the public has a limited memory for last month's news and is vulnerable to today's. When TV focuses on an issue, the public's priorities are altered, and then altered again as TV news moves on to something new.

This is not to suggest that the public behaves like a herd of sheep. Most people approach TV news with a good deal of skepticism. They check out how the news compares with other sources, and they tend to accept those views which agree with their own and to reject those which do not.

But it is far more important today than ever before that viewers watch TV "defensively." Viewers need to recognize the biases that are built into the present commercial television system. They need to compensate for the system's tendencies to support the status quo by relying on the views of those in power, both in government and business. They need to cultivate an even stronger habit of testing TV news — testing it against other sources of news, especially those that are noncommercial, such as the Public Broadcasting System in the U.S. and the semipublic CBC in Canada, and those that depend on citizen funding, such as subscriber-supported magazines and newspapers. They need to recognize the built-in bias of TV to reinforce the culture's own commercial values and worldview. And finally, they need to support reform measures that would help television support and enhance the political process rather than despoil it.

In sum, viewers must maintain *critical distance* between themselves and TV news, and then watch it from the perspective of their own worldview. For the Christian, this means viewing TV from the perspective of the Christian faith and its values and assumptions.

Unfortunately, we no longer can take TV for granted: "We are no longer fascinated or perplexed by its machinery. We do not tell stories of its wonders. We do not confine our television sets to special rooms. We do not doubt the reality of what we see on television, are largely unaware of the special angle of vision it affords."[12] Such easy acquiescence is hazardous to our health — both political and personal. We must not take TV for granted. We must constantly decide who is in control: TV or ourselves.

9

Media Imperialism: In Our Image

Freedom of speech has also become in practice the freedom of the rich.

           –Urho Kekkonen, President of Finland, 1980

In 1980 Anthony Smith, a TV producer for the BBC and a thoughtful analyst of the mass media, wrote a book called *The Geopolitics of Information: How Western Culture Dominates the World*.[1] His book was not alone. During the sixties and seventies more than a dozen works documented the increasing U.S. control over all forms of mass media production — especially news, broadcasting, advertising, and data flow — and thus its grip on the production of culture worldwide.

Smith's book is a balanced account, but it is still alarming. He points out that a kind of inevitability has been built into the West's view of the world, that during this century in particular we have believed it was our duty to bring to the rest of the world our religion, our products, and our way of life. He quotes the famous explorer and journalist H. M. Stanley, who, shortly after "finding" Dr. Livingston in the African Congo a century ago, returned to England to report to the Manchester Chamber of Commerce:

There are 500 millions of people beyond the gateway to the Congo, and the cotton spinners of Manchester are waiting to clothe them. Birmingham foundries are glowing with the red metal that will presently be made into ironwork for them and the trinkets that shall adorn those dusky bosoms, and

the ministers of Christ are zealous to bring them, the poor
benighted heathen, into the Christian fold.[2]

A hundred years later this crass commercialism and cultural
and religious paternalism embarrasses us. Yet today our newspapers and telecasts successfully obscure the fact that similar approaches to the third world have continued throughout the century following Stanley's remarks and continue still, with even
greater viciousness though greater subtlety.

The unleashing of the United States as a major world force
began right after the Second World War. Armed with more technology and production power than any other nation in history,
America began to exploit the worldwide potential for its goods
and services. At the same time, communication was beginning
to emerge as a major sector in the U.S. economy. Television
quickly developed into the most efficient sales device ever known.
The production of news and information became big business,
as more and more small town newspapers and even large city
independents became part of huge newspaper chains. The computer, developed during the war, became an essential element in
the growth of business. And the rocket, another war technology,
was put to use launching satellites that could girdle the earth
and provide a remarkably inexpensive way of sending information anywhere on the globe.

During this same period, colonized nations throughout the
world were beginning to throw off the political domination that
the Western nations had exercised during the century since Stanley and Livingston. Scores of countries, particularly in Africa,
declared their independence from European nations, which had
benefitted so richly from their natural resources. And so, during
the half-century since the Second World War, two global changes
were taking place simultaneously: power was shifting from the
European nations to the United States; and the third-world nations were asserting their political independence. What happened
next, in terms of world history and the behavior of nations, was
virtually inevitable, though morally thoroughly reprehensible: the
United States and its business community moved in to exploit the
weak and undeveloped third-world nations, which were no longer
"protected" by the British, Dutch, French, or Belgians.

The underdeveloped nations caught on quickly. By the 1950s
they realized that the old political colonialism was being replaced

by a new kind of economic colonialism. In 1956 they organized themselves as the "nonaligned" nations, asserting their independence from both capitalism (the first world) and communism (the second world). This "third world," as the group was called, began to press for a new economic environment that would protect them from being taken over by either the first- or second-world nations.

As they pressed for justice, one forum was the United Nations' Educational, Scientific and Cultural Organization (UNESCO). As the number of third-world nations increased, so did their voting clout in the U.N. and UNESCO. By 1970, at the Sixteenth General Assembly of UNESCO, a "New International Economic Order" was proposed. This concept was based on the idea that the third-world nations could not truly develop until they achieved economic independence from the first and second worlds.

By the 1970s communication also had become a major tool in the first- and second-world nations' attempts to recolonialize the third world. The United States already outstripped all other nations in development of communication technologies, and it was actively using its technological prowess to expand its domination of communication worldwide. The efforts of U.S. businesses, backed where possible by government money and power, were concentrated in four areas.

First, U.S. *news* dominated the entire world's daily output, and it continues to do so today. The Associated Press puts out some 10 million words overseas daily, serving 108 nations with 559 foreign correspondents and 62 foreign bureaus. United Press International produces some 11 million words and 200 news pictures overseas daily. Together, their output is approximately *ten times* the output of all the other press agencies — AFP (France), Reuters (United Kingdom), Tass (Soviet Union) and a half dozen others — taken together.[3] The resulting imbalance was perceived even by media executives. Roger Tatarian, a former vice president of United Press International, declared in 1978:

> There is in fact imbalance in the flow of news, both in content and volume, from the developed to the developing world. . . . It is true that this reflects the disposition of global military, economic and political power. Agency coverage often tends to seek simplistic solutions or Cold War ramifications in situations that are typically Asian, African or Latin American. . . . There is an acknowledged tendency

among Western media...to devote the greatest attention to
the Third World in times of disaster, crisis and confrontation.[4]

Second, U.S. *television* began to dominate the world scene, exporting some 200,000 TV programs a year, or more than twice
the number exported by all other nations combined. By 1974 a
UNESCO report found that only four countries were exporting
TV in any major way: the United States was annually exporting 150,000 hours of TV; the United Kingdom and France, about
20,000 hours each (including all the BBC programs on American
public broadcasting); and Germany about 6,000 hours. On the
other hand, the three U.S. TV networks were importing between
ten and twelve hours per year. In other words, while American
TV was importing the equivalent of two broadcast days' worth of
programming a year, they were exporting enough to fill the broadcasting schedules of twenty-two TV networks, operating eighteen
hours a day for a year! This dominance continues today, although
it is being slightly eroded by the emergence of several large multinational media producers outside the United States.

Third, U.S. *advertising* invaded virtually every nation of the
world, bringing with it values and images of indulgence and self-
centeredness. As early as 1965 Professor Harry Skornia was asking about the ethical implications of American advertising and
television programming sent into the third world:

Isn't the world we live in today so literally *one world* that
we can no longer be indifferent to poverty, hunger, and mis-
ery anywhere on the globe? And what effect on starving
people do our programs have — featuring waste, dissipation,
violence and luxury?[5]

One response to Skornia's question was supplied by sociologist
Alan Wells, referring specifically to burgeoning U.S. ads in Latin
America in the 1970s:

The effect of this type of programming is to encourage an
elite sector to live in North American style without the
sacrifices necessary for indigenous development, while the
masses are shown — but cannot enter into — the modern
cosmopolitan world. The content of such programs undoubtedly influences the viewer toward consumerism, without up-

grading his productive skills or increasing his willingness to save and sacrifice.[6]

Fourth, U.S. media domination focused on *data flow*, including control of the emerging new satellite transmissions. This is the least understood, yet potentially the most important form of cultural imperialism.[7] During the past four decades, communication has become increasingly a central component in all industries. Cees Hamelink estimates that 70 percent of the costs of industrial production today are devoted to the processing of information — research, market analysis, advertising, and internal company communications.

Some of the effects of U.S. data systems operating in other nations are almost bizarre. For example, when a Scandinavian city fire department decided to install an information retrieval system to give fire fighters instant read-outs of information about the fire-capabilities of any given address, they chose an American computer data base company because it entered the lowest bid. Now the Swedish fire fighters get the information they need, right down to the fastest route to the fire, instantly — via satellite, from Cleveland, Ohio.

The Failure of a New World Information Order

The third-world nations, recognizing that continuation of media domination made economic domination all the more inevitable, sought to buttress the UNESCO New Economic Order statement with a New International Information Order statement. In 1976 a UNESCO conference called for greater public access and participation in the media, for regional cooperation to develop news within the regions, and for agreement on the principle of a *"free and balanced flow"* of information. UNESCO appointed an International Commission for the Study of Communication Problems, under the leadership of Sean MacBride, former foreign minister of Ireland and a recipient of both the Nobel and Lenin Peace Prizes.

The commission's report, *Many Voices, One World,* was presented at the UNESCO Assembly in Belgrade in 1980. Immediately it came under attack from the Western nations, especially the United States. The large communication conglomerates rightly sensed in the report an attack on their unfettered exploitation of third-world markets. After strenuous negotiations at the Belgrade meeting of UNESCO, the sections which were most offensive to the West were removed, including: "the rights of peoples...to comprehensive and true information," "the right of each nation to inform the world about its affairs," and "the right of each nation to protect its cultural and social identity against false or distorted information which may cause harm." Finally the assembly agreed on a number of guidelines for a new information order, including: the elimination of the imbalances and inequities brought on by media monopolies; a "better balanced dissemination of information and ideas"; freedom of the press and of information; and respect for each people's cultural identity and its right to inform the world about its "interests, aspirations and social and cultural values."[8]

The response of the U.S. delegation revealed American opposition to the whole idea: "The resolution on the MacBride Report is largely what we had sought....It calls for widespread dissemination of the Report, for study and reflection, *but little concrete action as far as implementation is concerned*" (italics supplied).[9]

Still, the U.S. press reacted to the MacBride Report with rage — and considerable self-serving bias. A. H. Raskin, former assistant editor of the editorial page of the *New York Times*, conducted a study of U.S. papers during that period. He found some 448 news articles and 206 editorials dealt with the 1980 UNESCO Assembly. By far the most news stories — 39 percent — dealt with the debate over communications. Eighty-eight percent of the editorials were on this topic, and of these, 87 percent were strongly hostile. Twenty-seven newspapers urged U.S. withdrawal from UNESCO if it persisted in such actions. Raskin also reported that not *one* story coming out of the six-week conference dealt with UNESCO's battle against illiteracy, its development of alternative energy sources, its educational programs for scientists and engineers, its basic research into food production, and scores of other accomplishments during 1980. One might well ask whether the press's shoddy treatment of UNESCO exemplifies the very complaint — Western bias in the news — that led to calls for a New Information Order debate in the first place.

The U.S. press did not let up. They saw the UNESCO criticism of excessive concentrations of press control in the hands of a few huge Western monopolies, and the consequent "imbalances and inequalities" in news coverage, as a threat to their forty-year worldwide dominance of media. For months they railed against the so-called proposals "to license journalists," even though Recommendatìon Number 50 of the MacBride Report specifically states that "the commission does not propose special privileges to protect journalists in the performance of their duties, although journalism is a dangerous profession," and neither the UNESCO Secretariat nor any member state had formally advocated the licensing of journalists. Nevertheless, the press either chose not to understand what the UNESCO debate was really all about or purposefully misled the public about the matter; either way, the U.S. news industry adopted a less than "balanced" approach to the issue in order to protect its own self-interest.

In 1984 the U.S. unilaterally withdrew from UNESCO, calling the organization inefficient and unable to reflect the views of the larger nations. Great Britain was the only other nation that joined the U.S. in its protest. While some charges of inefficiency probably had merit, Colleen Roach, a former U.S. employee of UNESCO, wrote that the main argument used by U.S. officials to attack UNESCO was "its supposed intent of promoting government-controlled media."[10] The withdrawal of U.S. funds was nearly catastrophic to UNESCO; to placate the U.S., the UNESCO chief executive officer was replaced and its policies underwent a major shift. The U.S. had effectively destroyed the third world's challenge to worldwide media domination by U.S. media corporations.

To see what happens when the United States is able to bring so much of the world's culture into conformity with its own image, let us take a look at two case histories: the effects of U.S. media in the Caribbean and the recent American media campaign to sell cigarettes to the world.

Media Effects: The Caribbean

When Columbus discovered America — or to be more accurate, when the Arawak Indians on what we now call San Salvador discovered Columbus on their beach — a whole new world opened up to the Europeans (and, unfortunately, to these newly-named "Indians" as well!). The string of beautiful islands reaching from the north coast of South America to the "West Indies" (so named by Columbus in a miscalculation of some 12,000 miles) was soon colonized. Landowners from almost every Western European nation established plantations, imported slaves from Africa, and intermarried with the Indians.

When other parts of the third world were declaring their independence in the 1950s, most Caribbean nations joined in. But when first-world political domination ended, economic domination continued and even increased. Accompanying this new colonialism was domination over the access to news, information, and entertainment. Today, according to Allen Kirton of the Caribbean Council of Churches, "cultural penetration is the name of the game."

When a group of journalists and mission executives visited the tiny island of St. Lucia in 1988, Rickey Singh, a Caribbean journalist who edited the Caribbean Council of Churches' newspaper *Caribbean Contact*, greeted them with the words, "Welcome to the most media-penetrated region in the world." In the next few days, the group began to understand how media penetration works.

In the first place, all of the islands are small and pitifully poor. They cannot possibly afford to support quality television and radio productions. So some island governments simply set up satellite dishes to receive U.S.-based programs designed to feed U.S. and Canadian cable systems, and then they rebroadcast these pirated programs over a local TV channel. In many cases governments actually charge citizens a fee for the use of TV sets to receive the pirated American TV. Of course, along with the programs come news, commercials, and the North American weather. Consequently, the languages and customs and values of the Caribbean people are today being replaced with the language, customs, and values of commercial America. Alan Kirton described viewing "Life Styles of the Rich and Famous," a Popeye cartoon, "The Price Is Right," "The A-Team," "Miss Marple," "Miami Vice," "Crazy Like a Fox," the Jimmy Swaggart ministry, and a movie, "Charlie Grant's War," in a small Caribbean community and commented: "We have a Cadillac mentality in a bicycle economy." Testifying to the effects of such programs on the people of the tiny island of Montserrat, with a population of 12,000, and Saba, with only 1,000, he asked, "Where is my community in all that?" and he challenged North Americans to "consider the impact on these people!"

One example of what happens when communications come from outside the culture is the situation in Grenada. Marlene Cuthbart, a Canadian expert in communication studies and a long-time resident in the Caribbean, points out that Grenada, with a population of about 110,000, had a local TV station for ten years prior to the U.S. invasion. Following the invasion, in 1986, the

American government offered to help bring "Discovery TV," a U.S. satellite-fed system, to Grenada "to aid in development." Grenada could not easily refuse the offer. The system that arrived was privately owned by a Boston-based corporation. Soon the new manager, an American who persisted in wearing his cowboy hat on the hottest days, was overseeing construction of a down-link dish and "studio." However, the "studio" consisted of a single camera and a few tape recorders. There was no serious effort to provide local programming at all. The "studio" simply turned on the receiver, took the programming (including commercials) from North America, and sent it out over the TV channel. Coverage of the rest of the Caribbean was nonexistent. In fact, the famous annual Tobago Festival can be seen on TV worldwide — but not in Grenada, just a few miles away. What people in Grenada see is what people in Boston see — and they have no alternative.

A poet on the island of St. Lucia summarized their plight:

> If you change your language,
> You must change your life.

Imported television is changing not only the language but the whole life of the Caribbean. To be sure, there is a "free flow" of TV — a free-flowing, endless outpouring of sitcoms, music-TV, game shows and commercials, none of which were chosen by the people of the Caribbean, and none of which support their own customs, stories, and values — their own "language." One can begin to understand why the third world is trying so desperately to achieve a "balanced" flow of communication. They enjoy much that is available through first-world programming, but they also would like to have their own culture expressed, their own news heard, their own values affirmed. They call for justice — in this case, balance in the kind of communication they have access to.

Selling Cigarettes to the World

An even more distressing example of cultural imperialism is the recent media campaign by U.S. tobacco companies to increase their cigarette sales overseas. After the surgeon general of the United States reported that cigarette smoking was killing thousands of citizens each year and TV cigarette ads were banned in 1971, the number of smokers at first held steady and then began

to decline. Since 1981 U.S. cigarette sales have been going down
at a rate of about 2 percent each year. This decline has prompted
the industry to focus its advertising on potential new smokers —
women and youth.

For example, the amount of *visible smoke* in cigarette ads in
magazines has constantly decreased, to the point where in 1984
and 1985 no smoke was visible at all. Instead, the ads now associate cigarette smoking with health and vitality. For youth, they
sell adventure (sailing) and risk (rock climbing). For women, they
employ erotic images (romantic scenes on a yacht), and popularity (playing at a beach party). A recent study of tobacco ads
concludes: "In the face of increasing public knowledge about the
health risks of smoking and the shrinking population of current
smokers, the tobacco industry has portrayed smoking in advertisements in a misleading manner — as adventuresome, healthy,
safe, and erotic, images in stark contrast to the voluminous data
implicating smoking as a factor in ill health."[11]

But multinational corporations like R. J. Reynolds and Philip
Morris are not content merely to foul their domestic nest. With
the number of smokers continuing to drop at home, they found it
imperative to extend their sales overseas. The results have been
astonishing.

In 1988, C. Everett Koop, the U.S. surgeon general, released
the twentieth surgeon general's report on smoking, a 618-page
document which concluded that tobacco is as addictive as heroin.
Charged Koop, "Smoking is responsible for well over 300,000
deaths annually in the United States — more than 30 times all
narcotics-related deaths in the U.S. combined."[12] At the same
time, the Office of the United States Trade Representative in
Washington was putting economic and political pressure on the
governments of Japan, Taiwan, and South Korea to withdraw their
trade barriers and allow U.S. cigarette sales and advertising into
their nations.

Before American intervention in the Korean and Taiwanese
markets, both countries had near-total bans on tobacco advertising — no ads on TV, in newspapers, magazines, or even on
billboards. Japan had similar industry self-regulation. Now, because of U.S. trade threats, the American companies are allowed
to sell and advertise their cigarettes in all three nations without
even carrying the warnings on the packages that are required in
United States. Says Takeshi Hirayama, director of the Institute of

Preventive Oncology in Tokyo, "We grew up seeing the U.S. be-having like a leader of the developing world. Now we see their commercials for dangerous cigarettes." Hirayama says that when he lectures before Japanese medical societies he always gets the same question: Why are Americans trying to encourage Japanese to smoke? "I cannot think what to say. Some doctors say the ad-vertisements we have every night are an assault, like the old B-29 bombings. The term 'Ugly American' is coming back."[13]

The U.S. multinationals have a more difficult time in Europe, where they have faced severe restrictions on cigarette advertis-ing for years. There the solution has been *sponsorships*. Philip Morris has sponsored a racing car in the Grand Prix for more than a decade, and R. J. Reynolds has sponsored a car since 1987. This way, as with such sponsorships in the United States as the Virginia Slims Tennis Tournament, tobacco companies get their products on TV without "advertising."

However, Canada has managed to withstand the pressure. In mid-1988 Canada passed laws that ban all tobacco advertising and require cigarette packs to carry a detailed warning of the dan-gers of smoking — warnings that far exceed those in the United States. After 1993, all billboard and other outdoor advertising will be prohibited as well. How did this come about? First, about half of the nation's ten largest daily newspapers voluntarily stopped taking cigarette ads. Then smoking habits changed dramatically. Between 1982 and 1987 Canadian cigarette sales dropped 18 per-cent, while U.S. sales dropped only 8 percent. Garfield Mahood, executive director of the Canadian Non-Smokers' Rights Associ-ation, says, "The industry has had its legitimacy taken away. In America, they [the tobacco industry] still wrap themselves in the American flag."[14]

Indeed they do. In November 1987, Philip Morris, the U.S.'s largest tobacco company, sent a copy of *Pravda* to about five hundred newspaper editors. The cover letter read, "One world-famous newspaper without cigarette advertising." The letter went on to say, "*Pravda* does not carry cigarette advertising or indeed any advertising. Government control of information is typical of totalitarian regimes and dictatorships."[15] The mailing served lit-tle purpose, since virtually all U.S. newspapers regularly carry cigarette ads. But is *Pravda*-type control the only alternative? Peo-ple in Western Europe and Canada think not. They believe that it is possible to regulate commercial speech such as advertising and still maintain freedom of expression. And leaders in nations such as Japan, Taiwan, and South Korea wonder, too. They wonder why the United States, once a world leader in justice for the developing world, today allows its corporations to penetrate their cultures and to poison their people.

Reversing the Tide

There are signs of hope — places where men and women are working to reverse the tide of international media imperialism. Through their mission and communication agencies, many of the mainline denominations in the United States and Canada support the work of the World Association for Christian Communication (WACC), an ecumenical agency dedicated to increasing genuine communication in the underdeveloped nations. The WACC is governed by elected officials designated by all seven regions of the world — a truly democratic body where the third world has at least as much say as Europe and North America. With a staff of twenty located in Europe, this agency supports more than 150 communication projects in the third world.

For example, the Asian Social Institute in Manila illustrates how it is possible to reverse the tide of media domination. For twenty years the Philippines suffered under one of the most tightly controlled presses in the world. Whatever glorified the regime of Ferdinand Marcos was shown in the newspapers and on television; whatever was critical simply did not appear. In metropolitan Manila there is a large lake, more than a mile across. Prior to Marcos's imposition of martial law in 1972, the lake was a public fishing area supporting 70,000 people who lived around its shores. During the martial law years, the lake became "private," available only to large business interests and influential people in government. A cry for "justice" went up from the local fishermen — but they had no idea how to achieve justice.

The Asian Social Institute heard about the fishing community's problems. They taught local leaders how to develop their own newsletter. They showed local artists how to make posters that portrayed the local situation. They helped a group develop a slide presentation on the problem with a script written by the people themselves, incorporating their own poetry and songs. As the men and women grew more articulate in expressing their own problems, they developed the self-confidence to educate others and to take their plight to the whole community. They held a press conference. They began to generate support from lawyers, students, professionals, and church workers. They produced a daily local radio program, aimed at the fishing community, with local participants telling their own stories about the problem.

By the time President Marcos was overthrown in February 1986, the community leaders had developed enough skill and self-confidence to begin discussion with fishermen all over the country. In 1988 they organized a national congress, drafted a fisheries code that has been submitted to the Philippine Congress, and have been invited to various parts of the nation to train others in ecology.

This is but one example of *small group media* — the use of simple communication techniques to enable people to express their own ideas and needs and to gain the experience and confidence to use media to help bring about change.

The WACC supports this and similar projects, plus printing, broadcasting, and other media projects both large and small — all aimed at assisting the poor to free themselves from poverty and enslavement. Here is a concrete response to Paul's admonition to the Christians in Galatia: "For freedom Christ has set us free; stand fast therefore, and do not submit to a yoke of slavery" (Galatians 5:1).

Conclusion

We can summarize by saying that a relatively small number of corporations controls the production and distribution of communication throughout the world. These corporations are based primarily within the United States and other Western nations, and they are engaged in a kind of "peaceful invasion" of the third world, not to help poorer nations develop but to dominate them culturally and thus economically.

This rising tide of cultural domination can be turned back in two ways: through the support of efforts in the third world to achieve local communication that reflects local needs; and through reform of the media in the first world — which we will consider in some detail in Chapter 11, "What We Can Do."

The first Commandment forbids making images to worship instead of God. Perhaps a commandment for our media age should forbid us to make images in our *own* image, which we impose upon others in order to dominate and control.

10

Video Violence

Mother #1: "Don't let your kids see *Friday the 13th*; it's full of steamy sex."

Mother #2: "What? That's terrible! I thought it just had violence."
          —exchange overheard in Ridgewood, New Jersey

When Benjamin Spock, M.D., was starting out in pediatrics, he didn't believe that on-screen violence was harmful to children. Then, about thirty years ago, he changed his mind.

It was soon after *The Three Stooges* became popular on television. A nursery school teacher told Spock that suddenly children were beginning to bop each other on the head without warning. When she would tell a child who had just hit another that hitting wasn't acceptable, the child wouldn't show any regret but instead would say, "That's what the Three Stooges do."

Suddenly, Dr. Spock realized that children — especially young children — will pattern themselves after violent behavior just as readily as they will imitate good behavior. He realized that TV violence can cause harm to children.[1]

Sometimes it happens with adults, too. In 1984, after Farrah Fawcett played in *The Burning Bed*, a TV drama that told the true story of a battered wife who ended thirteen years of marital torment by setting fire to the gasoline-soaked bed of her sleeping husband, a number of copy-cat assaults occurred across the nation. In Milwaukee, thirty-nine-year-old Joseph Brandt viewed the TV show and shortly thereafter poured gasoline over his estranged wife and set her afire. In Quincy, Massachusetts, a husband became angered· by the movie and beat his wife senseless. In Chicago, a battered wife watched the show, and then shot her husband.[2]

It is a fact that people in the U.S. are more prone to violence than are people of any other industrialized nation. Between 1963 and 1973, while the war in Vietnam was taking 46,212 lives, firearms in the U.S. killed 84,644 civilians. If the United States had the same homicide rate as Japan, our 1966 death toll from guns would have been 32 instead of 6,855. In the last fifty years the rate of rapes in the United States has increased 700 percent, on a per capita basis. In 1980 there were eight handgun murders in England and 10,012 in the United States.[3] During the last thirty years the U.S. homicide rate per capita has increased almost 100 per cent. Between 1974 and 1983, the number per capita of aggravated assaults increased 6 percent, forcible rape 26 percent, robbery 2 percent, and child abuse 48 percent.[4] And although reliable Canadian statistics were not available before 1980, one authority states that "violent crimes have constantly increased" there during the last half-century.[5]

For years people have asked whether the amount of violence portrayed on movie and TV screens has anything to do with the growing violence in real life. As early as the 1950s, the U.S. Congress held hearings on the possible negative effects of television. Industry representatives immediately promised to reduce violence while simultaneously denying any evidence of harmful effects. Yet television violence increased steadily.

In 1967, following a two-week period when whole sections of Detroit and Newark were bombed, burned, and vandalized, President Lyndon B. Johnson established a National Advisory Commission on Civil Disorders. In March 1968, the Commission issued a 608-page report that laid much of the blame for the crisis on the mass media. The Commission charged that although the media tried to give a balanced and factual account of the events of the summer of 1967, they tended overall to exaggerate "both good and bad events." Television, in particular, was found to have presented violence in simplistic terms — depicting "a visual three-way alignment of Negroes, white bystanders, and public officials or enforcement agents," which tended to create the impression that the riots were predominantly racial confrontations between blacks and whites, while factors such as economic and political frustration were pushed into the background.

The national unrest persisted. In early 1968 Martin Luther King, Jr., was shot and killed in Memphis, then Robert Kennedy was assassinated in Los Angeles. A new U.S. National Commission on the Causes and Prevention of Violence, headed by Milton S. Eisenhower, stated: "Violence on television encourages violent forms of behavior, and fosters moral and social values about violence in daily life which are unacceptable in a civilized society." It concluded: "Television entertainment based on violence may be effective merchandising, but it is an appalling way to serve the 'public interest, convenience and necessity.'"[6]

Once again, the broadcasting industry resisted the conclusions of the Commission and attacked its findings as based on insufficient evidence. At the same time, network presidents solemnly proclaimed that violence *was* being reduced and that children's programming was being improved.

Yet one more time, in 1969, John O. Pastore, chairman of the U.S. Senate Communications Subcommittee, requested the surgeon general, Dr. Jesse Steinfeld, to appoint a committee to conduct a study "which will establish scientifically insofar as possible what harmful effects, if any, these [televised crime and violence] programs have on children." Steinfeld testified in 1972 at a Senate hearing that the study had unearthed "sufficient data" to establish a *causal relationship* between watching television violence and behaving aggressively. Said Dr. Steinfeld: "My professional response...is that the broadcasters should be put on notice. The overwhelming consensus and the unanimous Scientific Advisory Committee's report indicate that television violence, indeed, does have an adverse effect on certain members of our society."[7]

But according to the "Violence Profile" conducted annually by George Gerbner of the University of Pennsylvania's Annenberg School of Communication, the level of violence in television showed no significant change throughout the 1970s. Instead, broadcasters continued to insist that the research on behavioral effects of TV violence was "inconclusive."

The research continued, and in May 1982 the National Institute of Mental Health released the findings of a ten-year follow-up to the surgeon general's 1972 study: "After ten more years of research, the consensus among most of the research community is that violence on television does lead to aggressive behavior by children and teenagers who watch the programs."[8]

Thus by 1982 the overwhelming weight of research had demonstrated various degrees of relationship between violence in the media and violent behavior in the society. The U.S. public felt something was terribly wrong but lacked an organizational structure to do anything about the degree of violence. Some vigilante groups, tired of promises and no action by the broadcasting industry, began to take matters into their own hands by initiating boycotts and urging the passage of censorship laws in communities and states. Fortunately, they had very little success, because the courts rejected attempts by individual groups to impose their views on others.

At that point the National Council of Churches decided the time had come to do something about both the increase of violence and the increasing threats of censorship. But to take action, it first needed the facts. In 1983 it established a special study committee "to examine the problems of exploitative sex and gratuitous violence in the media."

The study had two aims: first to help church people and the public to identify the issues; and second, to identify solutions that would not restrict the rights of citizens to express themselves freely in a democracy.

The committee recognized that sexuality and violent actions are found in all of life, and that the mass media would be dishonest if it were to attempt to "sanitize" these dimensions of the human condition. For these reasons, the Commission focused on *"exploitative* sex" and *"gratuitous* violence."

In 1984 the study committee held three public hearings, one focused on the research findings (in New York City), a second on the views of the communications industry (in Los Angeles), and a third on policy proposals and alternatives (in Washington, D.C.). It heard testimony from thirty-one persons, including researchers, producers, directors, writers, actors, corporate executives, legislators, and leaders of national educational and public interest organizations.

Research Findings

The committee consulted some of the most respected and eminent researchers in the field. Here is a summary of what these experts reported.

Edward Donnerstein of the Center for Communication Research at the University of Wisconsin reported on young men who were exposed to "slasher" films (*I Was a Teenage Werewolf, Texas Chainsaw Massacre,* and *The Toolbox Murders*). When these men were placed in a "jury" at a mock rape trial, they were far more likely than the control group to believe that the rape victim "was asking for it," that the rape did not do serious damage to the woman, and that the accused should get off with a light sentence.

Donnerstein's research showed that films which combine erotic material with violence tend to *desensitize* people regarding aggression against women. He emphasized that the problem was with the element of *aggression,* not with the *sexual* component.

David Pearl of the National Institute of Mental Health had just conducted a ten-year follow-up study on behalf of the surgeon general's office. Pearl found that television has four effects on violent behavior:

1. direct imitation of observed violence;

2. "triggering" of violence which otherwise might be inhibited;

3. desensitization to the occurrence of violence; and

4. viewer fearfulness.

Regarding the overall social effect, Pearl warned:

> Consider the situation if even only one out of a thousand viewing children or youth were affected (there may well be a higher rate). A given prime time national program whose audience includes millions of children and adolescents would generate a group of thousands of youngsters who were influenced in some way. Consider also the cumulative effects for viewers who watch such programs throughout the year. Even if only a small number of antisocial incidents were precipitated in any community, these often may be sufficient to be disruptive and to impair the quality of life for citizens of that community.[9]

George Gerbner, dean of the Annenberg School of Communications, reported on the findings of his seventeenth annual Violence Profile, which indicated that the overall Violence Index during 1982–1983 once again had *not* diminished but was approximately at its seventeen-year average. However, violence in children's weekend programs reached a record *high*, with a rate of 30.3 violent incidents per hour against a seventeen-year average of 20. Gerbner summarized his findings:

> For the past 17 years, at least, our children grew up and we all lived with a steady diet of about 16 entertaining acts of violence (2 of them lethal) in prime time alone every night, and probably dozens if not hundreds more for our children every weekend. We have been immersed in a tide of violent representations that is historically unprecedented and shows no real sign of receding.[10]

Since then, Gerbner and his researchers have issued five additional annual Violence Profiles that show essentially the same pattern: no decrease in violence on TV. Indeed, there has been a slight but continuing *increase* in violent programming aimed at children through the 1987–1988 season.

Gerbner explained to the study committee the role of television in creating a "mean and violent world" in the minds of many viewers — particularly heavy viewers:

> Most heavy viewers in every education, age, income, sex, newspaper reading and neighborhood category express a greater sense of insecurity and apprehension than do light viewers....
> Fearful people are most dependent, more easily manipulated and controlled.... They may accept and even welcome repression if it promises to relieve their insecurities. That is the deeper problem of violence-laden television.[11]

Gerbner called for parents, educators, and religious and political leaders to mobilize, to combat not only violence in the media "but the larger structure of inequity and injustice behind it."[12]

The study committee concluded that violence in the media *does* lead to aggressive behavior by children, teenagers, and adults who watch the programs. The committee stressed that not all viewers become aggressive, of course, but the correlation between violence and aggressive behavior by some is undeniable. In the words of the committee: "Media violence is as strongly related to aggressive behavior as any other behavioral variable that has been measured."

Who's in Charge?

If media violence, especially when that violence is in its nature sexual, in fact does threaten the quality of American life, then how do the creative and managerial people in television feel about the use of violence in their productions? What pressures within the industry lead to such a high degree of violence? Who makes the decisions: the actors? directors? producers? distributors? networks? sponsors? And what can concerned citizens do about the problem?

These media issues were discussed by the National Council of Churches study committee with a number of the media creators in Los Angeles, people who spend most of their time bringing into being the world of television. What the committee found was disturbing, though perhaps predictable. First, individual members of the industry *are* concerned, many of them profoundly, about the increasing amount of sex and violence in the media in which they work.

For example, from Christine Foster, a major TV producer: "Mainstream, legitimate network and production company executives, producers, writers and directors, are, like you, conscientious citizens, family people, mothers and fathers....We are conscious of the effect we have on the public and on our communities."

Second, the people working in the media industries are part of a vast and complex system which parcels out responsibility, a little bit to everyone, so that, in the end, *no one is ultimately responsible*. For example, when participants in the Los Angeles hearing were asked, "Who has the responsibility to do something about the problem of sex and violence?" the answers consistently placed responsibility on *someone else*.

Actors said they only do what they are told by the writers and directors. Writers and directors said producers require them to put more sex and violence into the shows. The producers said it is the networks that demand more sex and violence. Networks said their choices are limited, the competition is brutal, and the sponsors demand results. Everyone agreed they don't like the amount of exploitative sex and gratuitous violence that they, together, created.

What about the sponsors? Producer Gene Reynolds charged

that "sponsors in the last twenty years have escaped responsibility." David Levy (president of the Caucus of Producers, Directors, and Writers) explained that some twenty years ago such sponsors as Kraft, Hallmark, and Texaco normally purchased a whole *series* of programs on television, but that today sponsors only purchase *time* — a few minutes of spot advertising on many different programs. Thus the sponsors now reach many different audiences many times each day but in doing so they diffuse their responsibility for any particular program among a half-dozen or more other sponsors.

Sponsors clearly have an interest in the content of programs with which the public may associate their commercial message. For example, General Motors has had the following guideline for many years:

> Our aim is to avoid association with those programs that appear to emphasize offensive subject matter and language for their own sake.

Levy summed up the situation by saying that "there are no 'wild men' in the media today. Instead, they are all in a System that traps them."

Third, each TV network has only one ultimate objective — to win the largest number of viewers during *every half hour of every day*. This ratings drive, on which fees for commercials are based, is the economic reality at the root of the problem.

Given this system, advertisers are acting quite rationally when they buy the cheapest programs that will reach the largest number of viewers with their message, regardless of program quality. Broadcasters are considered by their stockholders to be acting in an economically responsible way if they provide programs that are produced very cheaply — even if the programs contain much unnecessary violence — if, in doing so, they reach the largest possible audience and make the largest number of sales and highest possible profits. But their decision to air violent programs must be considered irresponsible by the public at large.

Deregulation of broadcasting in the U.S. and the Federal Communications Commission's apparent indifference to the practices of broadcast licensees and cable operators in effect seem to legitimize the operation of these media as businesses like any other business, disregarding the public trusteeship that is required by the Communications Act. In spite of the view of writer Bill Sackheim that "ninety percent of the people in this business want to do good work," the FCC has created a regulatory vacuum that inevitably fosters inexpensive, low quality programming which, to be cheap and yet get instant mass attention, must become increasingly violent.

In summary, there are four major reasons for the high amount of sexual violence and overall violence in TV produced in the U.S.: (1) monopoly control of program production and distribution by a handful of powerful companies; (2) the drive for profits far in excess of those enjoyed by the vast majority of U.S. businesses; (3) a lack of accountability on the part of sponsors; and (4) the failure of the Federal Communications Commission to exercise adequate oversight of broadcasting.

What has happened since the National Council of Churches study report and recommendations? Essentially nothing. The churches have not seen the issue as a high priority. Some even question whether church organizations ought to be meddling in such matters. The vigilante and boycott groups have gotten nowhere. Meanwhile, the Violence Profile for 1987 shows that the amount of violence on television continues at the same high levels. Some programming, such as MTV and cable channels, are actually increasing the overall amount of violence and sexual violence going into homes in North America.

What can be done? The study committee made specific recommendations for each of the major visual media in the U.S. — recommendations that remain to be implemented. In Canada the problems are somewhat different, both in scope and complexity. In May 1985 a Canadian Task Force report on Broadcasting Policy was established by the minister of communications, and it studied most of these same issues within the Canadian context.[13] Where applicable, the Canadian Task Force report will be used to supplement the U.S. recommendations.

How to Decrease Violence on Television

1. In the U.S., the key to decreasing violence on television is for broadcasters to exercise their responsibility to serve the public welfare. Television will serve this larger purpose only when the Federal Communications Commission reasserts its oversight of the broadcasting industry on behalf of the public interest. Broadcasting was deregulated during the early 1980s, and as long as deregulation remains in effect, the public cannot expect an industry engaged in a constant "business war" over ratings to take seriously its social obligation to reduce the amount of violence in its programming. The Canadian Radio-television and Telecommunications Commission (CRTC) regulates radio and television and imposes conditions of license which are considerably more detailed than in the United States. With the growth of the multinational communication giants and their effort to remove communication from regulation worldwide, Canadians should insist that present regulations of the CRTC not be compromised. Also, the Canadian Task Force recommends the creation of "TV Canada," a new satellite-to-cable service which would be non-commercial and would focus on "redressing the present imbalance that favours foreign [American] programs."[14]

2. In the U.S., broadcasting networks and stations should be required by the Federal Communications Commission to carry the rating of the Motion Picture Classification and Rating Administration (G, PG, PG-13, R, and X), with additional short descriptive phrases that indicate the amount and intensity of violence. Ratings and descriptions should appear in on-the-air promotions for programs, in newspaper and television guide listings, and in network, sponsor, and station advertisements.

In Canada, movie ratings are determined differently in each province, so there is no national rating system. However, the CRTC could enact a regulation requiring all stations to alert viewers to the amount and intensity of violence on forthcoming programs. Fortunately, many newspapers in Canada and the United States voluntarily note excessively violent and sexually explicit material in their movie reviews.

3. The FCC should be required to conduct annual hearings, open to the public, in which producers of television programming (networks, stations, syndicators, production houses, sponsors) would be required to explain how and by whom decisions are made to determine the content of entertainment programs. Only by such public discussion can the present anonymity of program decision making be penetrated and responsibility for program content be fixed. Stations should also be required to meet regularly with members of the public to discuss and assess the content and effects of entertainment programs and the relationships of these programs to generally accepted community values. Some stations follow this procedure even though regulations no longer require it, but most stations have dropped any significant community involvement.

4. Networks and stations should be required by U.S. law to devote a percentage of their air time, production budgets, and facilities to children's programming. The United States remains the only developed nation that does not require its television industry to provide programs for children. There is no Constitutional reason why Congress could not require television stations to provide regularly scheduled programming for children, Monday through Friday during after-school hours, at a time when older children could view it (4 p.m. to 6 p.m.). The courts have ruled that while the FCC cannot tell broadcasters *what* to broadcast, it can establish *program categories* that broadcasters must provide, and "children's programs" could be such a category.

In Canada the number of hours of children's programming per week actually increased between 1976 and 1985, but the CBC, Canada's public broadcasting network, recently has reduced its children's programming as part of overall cutbacks. If the Canadian Task Force recommendation for the creation of a "TV Canada" cable system is approved, the new channel would provide extensive additional programming for children and young people.

5. Incidents of violence should not be included in commercial announcements, such as trailers that advertise violent movies. If violent commercials are run, then free counter advertising time should be accorded to local community groups under a "Fairness Doctrine" which would require that a station that airs an issue of public importance (such as violence) must also air the opposing views. In the 1960s when the FCC required stations to run counter advertisements (under the Fairness Doctrine) every time an ad for cigarettes was played, the broadcasting industry soon agreed to legislation prohibiting all smoking ads, since the alternative was to run one *free* minute for every paid minute of cigarette advertising. The same mechanism could work against commercials with violence. In Canada, such additional regulation would be up to the CRTC.

How to Decrease Violence on Cable

1. The film rating system of the Motion Picture Association of America should be adopted by the U.S. cable industry. This step would involve a commitment by all "member" cable companies to make the ratings available in all advance information, schedules, and promotion as well as on the screen at the time of showing, as recommended for television broadcasting stations. In Canada, every cable company is licensed by the CRTC, which to date has much stricter requirements than in the U.S. The CRTC could require cable systems to adopt the MPAA ratings, or establish a similar rating system for Canada that would be carried on cable.

2. Congress should require all cable companies to make the lockout feature available on all channel-switching devices they normally provide to their subscribers. The lockout makes one or more channels temporarily unavailable.

3. Cable companies should be required to place all R- and X-rated films on a channel separate from other movies. For example, HBO, Cinemax, and The Movie Channel each would be required to have an "A" channel for family fare and a "B" channel for the more violent and sexually explicit films. This division would allow parents easily to lock out films deemed objectionable for their children, and still have access to them when desired. Suppliers such as Disney, which run only G, PG, or PG-13 films, would still have only a single channel, as would Playboy and other suppliers of exclusively R- and X-rated films. The advantage of this plan is that it does not restrict access on the part of adults while it gives parents more freedom of choice about what their children can see at home. The same system could work in Canada, especially since most of the "second tier" cable channels are American.

How to Decrease Violence in Videocassettes

The number of stores renting and selling videocassettes has increased dramatically during the past decade. Sixty percent of U.S. homes now have videocassette recorders, and this number is expected to increase steadily. The *New York Times* reports that dealers estimate that from 20 to 40 percent of cassettes rented in video stores are in the category of sexually explicit material. Virtually all of the R and PG-13 films that contain violent and sexually violent material are available for sale in videocassette stores. The situation is similar in Canada, and many of the video stores are subsidiaries of U.S. companies.

Congress should require that videos intended for adults (R-rated, X-rated, and unrated) not be displayed prominently in storefronts and not be sold or rented to persons under seventeen years of age. Videocassettes do not come into the home like cable

TV. Cassettes must be rented or purchased in stores. In this sense they are more like books or magazines than television, and they are entitled to the same protection under the First Amendment of the U.S. Constitution accorded books and magazines.

However, the First Amendment protection of free speech does not extend to children. The Supreme Court has taken the position that society has the obligation to judge what speech is appropriate for children. Just as persons under a certain age are not allowed to drink, drive, or vote, the sale of X-rated videos to children should be forbidden, either by industry self-regulation or, if this does not work, by law. Most video stores in the U.S. and Canada do not openly display X-rated videos, or sell or rent them to children under seventeen. On the other hand, to allow government the authority to decide what *adults* may see and hear represents a greater threat to the welfare of the society than to allow expressions that may be objectionable to many.

Conclusions

Clearly, violence and sexual violence in the media must be reduced. This goal can be attained without depriving those in the media of their livelihood or the rewards which are justly theirs, and without depriving citizens of their freedom of speech.

In Canada, the Canadian Radio-television and Telecommunications Commission is reasonably responsive to public concerns, and concerned citizens should express their views regarding the growing problem of violence and sexual violence in all of the mass media. The CRTC could require better information about the amount of violence in broadcast material; it could insist that the CBC and other broadcasters provide more children's programming; and it could require lockout boxes on all cable systems — changes that would go a long way in dealing with violent material.

In the U.S., concerned citizens must understand the extent to which the whole *system* of commercial broadcasting establishes an environment encouraging not violent programming itself, but the conditions that result in violent programming. Profits require large audiences and economies of production. Large audiences require vivid, exciting, simple movement. Economies of production require stereotypes and action rather than complex relationships. Sponsors want audiences, networks engage in "business war," and writers and directors get the message: more violent action.

In one sense no one is in charge of this complex system, hence no one can be blamed. But in another sense, *everyone must share the blame* — including the audience, the industry, and the political leaders who symbolically wash their hands of the problem by leaving it to "the marketplace." So long as we allow television to be an instrument for sales rather than for communication, the situation will persist. Christians have an obligation to reduce violence wherever possible, an obligation that stems from the explicit teachings and example of Jesus, from their faith in God's purpose for human creatures to live in harmony, and from their everyday ministry with those who suffer the effects of violence.

In the next chapter we will look in more detail at what concerned Christians can do about the problem of violence as well as other problems in the media, through media reform.

11

What We Can Do

> Give me the liberty to know, to utter, and to argue freely
> according to conscience, above all liberties.
> —"A Speech of Mr. John Milton for the Liberty of
> Unlicensed Printing to the Parliament of England," 1644

What can we *do*? How can we interpret the gospel today? How
can we use the mass media responsibly? How can we deal with
cultural values and worldviews that are so at odds with Christian values and the Christian worldview? What can we do about
the news distortions, the media imperialism, the misleading TV
religions, the video violence?

The answers fall roughly into three categories: using the
media, reforming the media, and understanding the media. In
Chapter 7 we have discussed some ways Christians can use the
media for authentic mission and witness. Now let us look more
closely at media reform and intentional media education.

Reforming the Media

Media reform is a task for Christians, but it certainly is not their
task alone. The idea that communication in our lives must be
open, diverse, and free-flowing if we expect to participate fully
in the human race and all its potential must capture the imagination of every person who wants TV to fulfill its possibilities
for enjoyment and enlightenment, every mother and father who
is concerned about the way her or his children will grow up, and
every citizen who wants her or his nation to be a place of freedom and hope. Without reform in the present way the media are

functioning, these things cannot be. Holding and communicating ideas is essential to our being free citizens. As Christians, with our commitment to helping set humans free from every kind of bondage, we join other citizens in this fundamental issue. And it is only by acting together, as Christians and non-Christians, that we can do anything significant about maintaining this freedom.

As we have described, various economic and political powers have conspired to control people's ideas by dominating the media that inform them. And, especially during the last fifty years or so, the media have become so massive and at the same time so susceptible to control by a few, that the danger of dominance has increased manyfold. It is increasing even today. That danger can be summed up in one word: *monopoly*.

Media monopoly is most visible when the control is exercised by government. We can thank God that in our countries controls of this nature are limited to a few situations, such as the abuse of "Top Secret" designations by some government officials to protect their own power. But media monopoly is not nearly so visible when exercised through economic means, through power wielded by large corporations. It is this second kind of monopoly which those of us in the United States and Canada should fear the most, and against which we must protect ourselves — through media reform.

During the last quarter century, the large mass media corporations themselves have been taken over by even larger corporate powers. Today the top 500 corporations in the U.S. own most of the 50 largest media companies, including 7 of the 20 largest newspaper chains and all 3 major TV networks.[1]

Ben Bagdikian, author of *The Media Monopoly*, says that when he wrote his book in 1983 he was concerned that "the majority of all major American media — newspapers, magazines, radio, television, books and movies — were controlled by fifty giant corporations." But in his introduction to the second edition, in 1987, he notes that the number of corporations controlling the media had dropped from fifty to *twenty-nine*.[2]

Bagdikian explains why this centralization is so dangerous:

> In the past, each medium used to act like a watchdog over the behavior of its competing media. The newspaper industry watched magazines, and both kept a public eye on the broadcasting industry.... But now the watchdogs have been

cross-bred into an amiable hybrid, with seldom an embar-
rassing bark."[3]

Close ties between the corporate world and the media can affect content in rather subtle ways: "The most powerful influence,
possessed by all [media corporations], is the power to appoint
media leaders. It is a rare corporation that appoints a leader considered unsympathetic to the desires of the corporation.... Real
independence for a media subsidiary is, at best, a disposable
luxury."[4]

Consider, for example, what can happen when Time, Inc., a
huge media empire that owns not only *Time*, *People*, and *Sports
Illustrated*, but also several book publishers, a cable and television group that includes 767 cable franchises, and much more,
merges with Warner Communications, which owns TV stations,
cable systems, book publishers, and a major Hollywood film studio. Theoretically a book could be published in hard-cover by
Little, Brown (a division of Time, Inc.), then be "selected" by the
Book-of-the-Month Club (owned by Time, Inc.), be given a rave
review in *Time* magazine, then issued in paperback by Warner
Books, made into a motion picture by Warner Bros., turned into
a TV series by Warner Television, and have a guaranteed run on
hundreds of cable TV channels. Bagdikian predicts that "it is quite
possible that by the 1990s a half-dozen large corporations will
own all the most powerful media outlets in the United States."[5]

Clearly, the treatment of media independence as a "disposable
luxury" can affect the creation and marketing of entertainment,
and the same process can occur in the treatment of news and
all kinds of information. But how does media monopoly affect
the public welfare? If the system is more efficient, what is the
harm in having fewer sources of communication? In a famous
letter written in 1787, Thomas Jefferson declared that, if he were
able to decide whether a people should have a government without newspapers or newspapers without a government, he would
not hesitate to prefer the latter:

> I am persuaded myself that the good sense of the people
> will always be found to be the best army. They may be led
> astray for a moment, but will soon correct themselves.... The
> basis of our governments being the opinion of the people,
> the very first object should be to keep that right.[6]

Today our concern to maintain freedom of the press and free speech must take into account new ways that the right of people to form their opinions can be limited. If a "book" can be created and merchandised from rough draft to a major motion picture and TV series by a single monopoly interest, surely "ideas" can be created and merchandised the same way. Monopoly control of the mass media, exerted not by government but by business, can have a devastating effect on our culture.

What can we do about it? How can we keep the media open, free, and expressive of the ideals that truly represent the people who make up the North American culture? In Chapter 9 we discussed video violence. Dealing with violence provides one good example of what people can — and cannot — expect to achieve in reforming the media. The NCC study committee gave considerable thought to "what should be done" about violence in TV, in motion pictures, in cable and videocassettes. And the first point is: *there are many different media, and they require many different tactics.*

Television

Television, one of the worst offenders, is a medium that can be regulated. As we have said, broadcasters have a special obligation in return for their special privileges. They are allowed into every home, and they have exclusive use of a valuable limited frequency. In return they are *required* by law to broadcast "in the public interest."

In Canada this requirement still is taken seriously by the government's regulatory commission. But in the U.S. the requirement is a well-kept secret. So effectively has the U.S. broadcast industry hidden behind the First Amendment that they have persuaded the public to think that the Constitution intended to protect the broadcasters rather than the public. But the Supreme Court has made it abundantly clear that in broadcasting, it is the public who has rights and broadcasters who have responsibilities. In its famous *Red Lion* decision, the Supreme Court said, "It is the right of viewers and listeners, not the right of broadcasters that is paramount."[7] This means that when freedoms conflict, the right of the public to news, information, or entertainment is more important than the right of the broadcaster to make money or even to speak out on issues.

This bring us to the second major point: *in the U.S. broadcast-*

*ing must once again be regulated in the public interest; in Canada
it must continue to be regulated.* Deregulation of broadcasting is
offensive because it removes the broadcaster's accountability to
the public. The deregulation in the United States over the past
decade has not worked well in other areas, either: in the stock
market it brought on a rash of scandals; in the airlines it resulted
in poorer service, higher prices, and the end of service to many
smaller cities. And the recent decision in Canada to deregulate
many aspects of the marketplace and increase U.S. trade has made
that nation much more vulnerable to American economic exploitation. Deregulation of heavy industry's air pollution has resulted
in acid rain and dying lakes in both nations. But in some ways
broadcasting deregulation is the most serious, because it places information — the *minds* of people — into the hands of those whose
first interest is profit. When that happens, we may never again
be able even to *know* about things like acid rain and dying lakes,
unless we see them for ourselves, first-hand.

One principle of broadcast licensing is that the public should
be able to challenge a station that is not broadcasting an adequate
amount of news, public affairs, minority or children's programs.
But how can the public challenge stations if there are no minimum
requirements? And how can people even know what stations are
doing if the stations no longer have to keep records or make them
available to the public? We know, roughly, the results of media
deregulation in the U.S. We know that from 1982 to 1987 ads-
per-hour on nationwide TV increased 14 percent.[8] We know that
shortly after deregulation, all three major networks fired everyone
in their religious TV departments and almost completely eliminated all public service religious programming. We know that in
1984 in Chicago, for example, the ABC affiliate moved all its public affairs programs to the 6:00–8:00 a.m. time slot — and scheduled Rock Video on Sunday mornings from 8:30 to 10:00 a.m.
We know that because crossownership of media restrictions were
removed, a single huge conglomerate may now own TV, radio,
cable, and newspapers — all in the same community, which gives
it unprecedented political power. As Jack Valenti, head of the
Motion Picture Association of America, said at the time deregulation began: "Whoever controls television controls public opinion.
Nobody, not even Saint Francis of Assisi, should be given that
power."[9]

Until deregulation is rolled back, the reforms suggested in

these chapters simply have no real chance of succeeding. So long as deregulation is in effect, local public interest groups who have difficulty getting stations to meet their demands for reasonable reform should consider petitioning the FCC to deny the license of the station. This approach was used with considerable success during the sixties and seventies. It requires considerable time, money, and expertise, but a station takes nothing more seriously than a carefully crafted petition to the FCC, and sometimes the mere threat by those in positions of moral authority is sufficient to get stations to meet their public service obligation more effectively. A word of caution, however: citizen groups must never abuse their privilege by attempting to dictate *what* is said on the air. Maximum exchange of ideas and views and an increase of service in various categories such as news, information, and children's programming, not censorship, must be the objective.

Motion Pictures

Motion pictures are a different medium with different legal restraints. People go out to the movies. They pay to see a film. Therefore, it requires different strategies, with an emphasis upon *industry self-regulation* rather than government licensing. Since almost all films seen in Canada are made in the United States, the approaches here will deal with the U.S. motion picture industry:

1. The present Motion Picture Association of America (MPAA) rating system should be improved by the addition of simple, short phrases that explain why a particular rating is given. Words such as "brief frontal nudity," "strong sexual language," "mild comic violence," "Western violence," or "strong graphic violence" would accompany PG, PG-13, R, and X ratings, and would help parents decide which films are suitable for their children.

2. Local churches should join with other community groups in establishing panels for review and evaluation of movies playing at local theaters, and in helping communicate any resulting viewpoints to church members and others in the community. For example, brief reviews and recommendations can appear in church newsletters and local newspapers.

3. Local churches should initiate processes for analyzing movies appearing in their communities through viewing and dis-

cussing them from the perspective of the Christian community. Adult film education is an important part of the responsibility of local churches.

Cable

Cable TV, on the other hand, presents different problems with different solutions. Cable comes into the home only if it is purchased. For the movie channels, the most likely source of violence, fees beyond the basic service rates are required. Again, in Canada most of these "second tier" services consist of U.S.-made films.

Ultimately, cable operators should be required to act as *common carriers*. That is, they should be given a monopoly to use the city streets to wire the homes of a community, but in return they should be required to carry all kinds of services — news (Cable News Network), information (The Weather Channel, Financial News Network), entertainment (Home Box Office, Cinemax), sports (ESPN), children's programming (Disney), ethnic programming (Spanish Information Network, Black Entertainment Television), and religion (VISION-TV in Canada, VISN in the U.S.). All cable companies would charge a fair price, established by the state public service commission (like gas and electric rates). All would be required to increase the number of channels as the demand increased, so the more services that were offered, the more profit the cable operator would make. But the cable operator would not also be a programmer or be able to choose which channels can get on a cable system, as is sometimes the case now.

If this arrangement had been established twenty years ago, as some public interest and church groups urged, today we would have much more diverse programming on cable. Cable companies would not be able to freeze out some program suppliers in favor of others in which they have a financial interest. Common carrier status for cable still can be achieved, especially if existing telephone companies are allowed to compete by bringing their own fiber optic "cable" into the homes they already serve. A proposal similar to "common carrier" status for cable operators was made in 1986 by the Canadian Task Force on Broadcasting Policy, but it has not been implemented.

Videocassettes

Finally, videocassettes present a major problem, not only because the number of cassette players has increased so dramatically but also because videos are bought or rented, and are therefore legally treated more like books. The NCC Study Committee made the following recommendations regarding videos:

> Videos intended for adults — R-, X-rated, and unrated — should not be displayed prominently in store-fronts. They should not be sold or rented to persons under 17 years of age. To take more restrictive action, the Committee believes, would unduly restrict the First Amendment rights of adults. (Citizens in a local community could use various levels of persuasion with the video store owner: consultation, letters to the local newspapers, appeals to the city council to make zoning changes, or stage actual public protests or a boycott.)

Other Strategies for Media Reform

Two important strategies are open to citizen groups. One is *corporate stockholder action*. Often the most effective approach to economic power is countervailing economic power. Businesses listen when their profits are threatened. For example, a few years ago in the U.S. several denominations and the National Council of Churches organized a protest in the stockholder meetings of several corporations that advertise on high-violence TV programs. As a result, a dozen major advertisers agreed to avoid sponsoring ads on high-violence programs.

The difficulty was that in response to the pressure to reduce violence, Hollywood began to increase the amount of sexual titillation. What is needed is continuous, well-thought-out pressure maintained over several years. If the churches could agree on such a strategy, the amount of violence and sexual violence might be reduced considerably.

The other strategy is the *boycott*. This tool is powerful, but dangerous, and to be used only after all persuasive and legal alternatives have failed. Even then, a boycott requires extreme caution, because it is a blunt tool that may hurt innocent people and have many unforeseen consequences. For example, when an organization led by Donald Wildmon waged a boycott campaign against 7-Eleven Stores in an attempt to get the chain to stop selling *Playboy* and *Penthouse* magazines, many local franchise holders were hurt. Meanwhile, other nearby stores reported that their sales of these two magazines soared. Thus, while the local 7-Eleven franchise holder may have suffered, the real objective — to get people to not read *Playboy* and *Penthouse* — was not achieved. (In fact, some suggest that both magazines may have benefitted from the publicity.) Stockholder action is far more sensible and effective. However, neither stockholder action nor boycotts should be used to censor specific speech, but to encourage the development of *more diverse* speech.

Beginning with the Moral Majority in the early 1980s, a number of groups have sprung up that appeal to Christians to join in boycotts of "offensive" words, pictures, stories, and so on appearing on TV and in other media. On the whole, the focus of those groups tends to narrow into a demand for censorship. A good rebuttal to these attempts to get good people to join in these narrow censorship-type movements is the statement by ACT, Action for Children's Television, which circulated a petition in 1981 that said, in part:

> Because we feel that the methods used by the Moral Majority and the Coalition for Better TV threaten the free exchange of ideas in a free society....
>
> Because we are offended by the narrow views of Moral Majority leaders who judge those who disagree with them as un-Christian and immoral....
>
> We...express our deep concern and protest over the... crusade now being conducted by the Moral Majority and the Coalition for Better TV to purge television of program content they deem offensive. We support citizen action to expand television viewing options for the American public, particularly for children.
>
> We believe, however, that the censorship tactics of the Coalition for Better TV limit options and threaten the free exchange of ideas in a free society.[10]

There are positive, rather than negative strategies, that can bring about reform of the media. Here are a few that merit consideration by concerned Christians:

1. Support public broadcasting. Local public TV and radio are a great untapped resource in many communities. They can be encouraged to produce more local programming, and local church leaders can provide ideas, resources, and programming, so long as the programs deal with "public service" rather than proselytizing.

For example, WTVS-TV, the public TV station in Detroit, has a community center in the station to encourage local productions, provides a twenty-four-hour-a-day job listing on local cable TV, provides an "electronic town meeting" on many local community issues, and has several local storefronts with TV cameras for local input. More than 700,000 households watch WTVS every week. Churches could encourage *any* public station to provide the same services to help develop community in their city or town, regardless of size.

2. Give awards for service of merit: annual awards to the best public service programs on local TV; special "Service Citations" to media leaders in the community; a prize for the best local TV or cable program in the community.

3. Provide a review service for the local newspaper. Reviews could be written by a well-known local figure who can be even-handed and reliable. The reviews need not be "Christian" to be a valuable information service to the community.

Education for Media Consumption

Professor Hidetoshi Kato of Gakushuin University in Tokyo says that in Japanese folklore the mammal called a tapir is the "animal who eats dreams." But, says, Prof. Kato, "I am inclined to think that human beings are now transforming themselves into tapirs."

As we have seen, people "consume" news and information because they *need* it, daily, almost hourly, as a source of how people behave, should behave, can behave. People consume news because it informs our daily moral routine, recharges our faith in an ordered world, and so helps us to get through another day. Indeed, as Prof. Kato says, "information is a kind of food, indispensable for many of our contemporaries. Many of us simply cannot survive without information."[11]

But we are not yet sophisticated enough to consume information and images in ways that are of maximum benefit to our health. Most of us do not have the visual literacy to understand visual statements. Our image-eating habits are still very primitive and indiscriminate. We eat everything — and then wonder why we suffer from indigestion.

Media education has only just begun to be taken seriously in the United States and Canada. Canadians have maintained a slight lead over efforts in the United States, partly because several of the early gurus of mass media, including Harold Innis and Marshall McLuhan, taught in Canada, and partly because Canada has a long tradition of media responsiveness to public interest, including the National Film Board and the Canadian Broadcasting Corporation. But in both nations the predominant educational systems have pretty much ignored media education, except for a few "honors" classes in high school. And the churches have continued to function as though the communication revolution had not occurred, except that sermons have mysteriously shortened as the attention span of most people, re-shaped by TV, has continued to decrease.

However, if we are going to learn to come to grips with the most powerful influence in our lives, we will have to take our heads out of the sand. Children should be taught to "read" television, starting in kindergarten. By the time they reach mid-elementary levels, they should be discussing many of the topics considered in this book, including the hidden meanings behind symbols and signs, and they should be learning the "language" of visuals, such as close-ups, fade-outs, and editing — and producing their own statements using cameras and editing equipment. When they are in high school they should learn more sophisticated aspects of the media: who's in control, how the power is exercised, how advertising and profits affect what is covered in the news and what is said in all programs, how viewing violence affects us, and how our media imperialism affects other people.

But this is not all. Values don't just exist; they are learned. Schools should also help our children understand the values carried in the media. Our culture includes Shakespeare and Longfellow, but today it also includes such classics as *Silent Spring* and *Catcher in the Rye*. Our educators know this. But somehow they do not know — or admit — that our culture includes "Star Trek" and "MASH" — and that these are classics as well. Such media programs carry values, they yield insights, they have tremendous resonance among both thoughtful and popular elements of the audience. And even the "negative" programs on TV — the game shows and "Miami Vice" and Music TV — should be included in the curriculum, so that students will begin to understand their culture and become capable of separating the good from the bad from the indifferent.

The churches in Canada and the United States have two responsibilities in media education. First, they should pioneer in general media education, pointing the way for public education. The church has always moved into areas of need where the rest of society was not yet ready to move. In the nineteenth century the churches created dozens of colleges and universities to meet the pressing need for higher education. Today understanding our culture is just as pressing a need. Churches could provide the courses — for children, young people, and adults — that would help millions of people begin to work their way out of frustration and bafflement at being confronted with something they do not understand: today's mass media.

Second, churches have always been in the forefront of values education. Ethics is a central task of religious education: to help people separate good from bad, right from wrong, the positive from the negative. Never has this task been more crucial than it is today, and few subjects are more in need of ethical reflection. Therefore, values education, dealing primarily with the visual media such as television, holds tremendous potential for educating Christians. And the media itself offers the way: videocassettes. Imaginative and exciting education, with specific courses targeted to children, youth, and adults, dealing with Christian values and how they relate to current TV, film, and video, is tailormade for videocassette distribution to churches, schools, and families.

Finally, here are a few suggestions about what people in local churches can do. Since each community and church has different needs and different capabilities, these are suggestions only. You will have to fill in the details.

1. Produce low-cost videocassettes of the worship service that can be taken to shut-ins. Or take a worship video to your local cable system for distribution on Sunday morning.

2. Develop a curriculum in your church school classes that deals with Television Awareness Training.*

---

*Ben Logan, ed., *Television Awareness Training: The Viewer's Guide for Family and Community* (Nashville: Abingdon, 1979); other materials are available from United Methodist Communications, 475 Riverside Drive, New York, NY 10015. Also contact *Media and Values*, 1962 Shenandoah St., Los Angeles, CA 90034, for media awareness education materials.

3. Hold film discussion groups for adults, based on films at the local movie theaters. Or have "intergenerational" discussion — adults and teenagers.

4. Base a Bible study course on the gospel and the media.

5. Generate a write-in campaign regarding a particularly bad —or good — example of television. Write the local station, network, producer, sponsor.

6. Invite a local TV or radio station manager or programmer to an adult class or a Television Awareness Training session.

7. Refer to television programs as illustrations for sermons and talks.

8. Develop an affordable local church day care program for children — instead of encouraging parents and others caring for children to use TV as their "baby sitter."

9. Make the church available after school for children who otherwise would be spending their time with TV; provide tutoring, play activities, reading.

10. Involve kids in making and discussing their own videos as a way of becoming literate with television. Set up a "lab" for shooting, editing, producing news, educational or arts programs.

11. Include a discussion of media and values in membership training.

12. Use local radio, television, or cable to help build community: encourage coverage of local issues.

13. Make a video to interpret the work of the church to its members: a stewardship video.

14. Raise the "media issue" in meetings with church school teachers, with education, mission, and stewardship groups.

15. Develop a program in the church on human relations and sexuality, using examples of the cultural problem that can be found on videos.*

---

*Copyright laws limit ways videocassettes can be taped and viewed with groups. In the U.S., see "Video Copyright Guidelines for Pastors and Church Workers," pamphlet by Jerome K. Miller, available from the National Council

16. Publish reviews in the parish bulletin: reviews of TV, movies, books, music albums. Or use the church bulletin board.

17. Produce a telephone call-in meditation for the day; talk with your local telephone company for details.

18. Develop a "TV Diet" that helps parents plan with their children how to restrict television viewing to certain programs and times.

19. Discuss the culture-media issue in local area pastors' meetings.

20. Establish a "resource center" as part of the church library. Create a library of videos for check-out and use in members' homes: on parenting, marriage enrichment, Bible study, and so on.

21. Teach a course in myth (for adults, teens, or children): help them tell their own stories, then understand myths of the Bible versus those of the present culture.

22. Using current examples from TV, teach a course on one of the following: news, children's programming, how to view TV, sexuality, or violence.

23. Encourage the development of a course in media literacy in your public school system: at elementary, junior high, and high school levels.

Whatever you do, be careful not to make media education simply the newest fad. Thoroughly integrate your actions into the ongoing work in the church. The idea is to help us as congregations carry what we experience on Sundays out into our Monday-through-Saturday lives — to help all of us understand *our* story as Christians in the context of the stories we encounter in the media every day.

---

of Churches, Room 860, 475 Riverside Dr., New York, NY 10115. In Canada copyright law is in transition. Consult about educational use of videos with a denominational resource center or a public library.

Conclusion

Which Is to Be Master?

> My prayer is not that you take them out of the world but
> that you protect them from the evil one.
> —Jesus' farewell discourse to his disciples (John 17:15)

As the dominant mythmaker of our time, television has come a
long way from what Newton Minow called the "vast wasteland"
of the 1960s. Public broadcasting, especially in Canada, has created educational programs for children that have great appeal.
For adults there are lessons in cooking, French, gardening, home
repair, and even dog training. Nature programs expand our understanding of the earth and its wonders. Some of the world's most
insightful thinkers come into our living rooms on a regular basis.
Great music and plays are available almost every evening.

At the same time, commercial television is a disgrace. Especially in the U.S., both local and network news is simplistic and
presented with a "happy face" geared more to entertainment than
enlightenment. The torrent of commercial appeals never ends.
Children's programs are often full-length commercials. Nighttime
network programming manages each year to reach new lows in
common-denominator fare. As the amount of violence increases,
the quality and amount of news and issue analysis diminishes.
And commercial cable brings language and actions into our homes
that we would not condone for adults visiting in our homes, much
less for our children. Here we have the problem in a nutshell.
The mass media could be a positive, humanizing force in our
lives but it is not, because the *culture* to which we belong has
the wrong values and worldview. The culture, through the mass

media, is cultivating the *wrong myths*. The media promote luxuries, encourage waste, and praise the life of things, while the gap between the rich and poor increases both within and between nations. Technology — "what works" — has become our god, expressed in all the most powerful myths of the most powerful media, while the God of justice and love is relegated to the sidelines of life, expressed in antiquated language and obscure stories lacking both clarity and relevance.

However, the current state of the media and its myths does not have to be our future fate. Just because technology is *possible* does not mean that it is *inevitable*. Consider a recent speech by the chairman of Eastman Kodak to that corporation's shareholders, which unwittingly reveals that people, not technology, finally can have the upper hand:

> About ten years ago, the continuous wave dye laser was invented during research at Kodak....But Kodak has never produced such a laser for market, and so far we have no plans to do so. That market has never had the earnings potential to justify the cost of developing it.
>
> I think the point is clear. Just because Kodak knows *how* to make a product doesn't mean that we *should* make it.[1]

Just because the media are dehumanizing in so many ways does not mean that they *must* continue that way. The media can be reformed. Its myths can be changed. People can learn how to protect themselves from media myths that are distortions and falsehoods. And nations can establish laws that protect their citizens from media monopoly and hence media domination.

While it is true that we are shaped by the technology we purport to control, the solution is not to withdraw from all technology. Rather, the solution is to work *through* the problem, to insist on shaping the technology which threatens to control us. We are back to the famous debate between Alice and Humpty Dumpty:

> "The question is," said Alice, "whether you can make words mean so many different things."

> "The question is," said Humpty Dumpty, "which is to be master — that's all."

We must think of the media less as acting upon us, and more

as being acted upon *by us*. It is the structure of the culture that
acts upon the media and, in a sense, tells it what to say. And
that culture is *our* creation. True, we inherit a great deal of our
culture. But we also can change it.

The task of Christians regarding the gospel, culture, and media
is to work toward changing culture so that it serves the needs
of people in the light of the gospel's myths — in particular, the
need of people for love and justice. The mass media must cease
being the willing slave of the capitalist spirit and instead become
subservient to human needs.

In A.D. 1400, more than a thousand years after Ptolemy developed the model that put the Earth squarely in the middle of
the universe, astronomers were still bending and stretching that
old "explanation" to fit their own observations, which told them
it just was not so. A painful struggle was required to change a
culture's perspective to see that the Earth merely revolves around
the sun. Today, more than three hundred years after John Locke
spelled out his theory that the greatest good is served by each
person following his or her own best interests, some economists
and politicians are still trying to bend and stretch this outmoded
"explanation" of life to fit social realities that say it just doesn't
meet human needs today.

The legacy of John Locke's philosophy is the capitalist spirit
and the dependency upon technology — theories that place efficiency and profits above human fulfillment. That worldview
solves problems with marvelous efficiency, but it also brutalizes
the weak and robs the poor. The gospel we have been examining
challenges that worldview. Instead, the gospel proposes a worldview in which men and women are the children of God, and
where human growth and development is a far more important
goal than the possession of any power or thing. The gospel insists that human beings are the greatest good, and that everyone's
needs are best met when we live in community, caring for each
other rather than looking out for Number One.

This worldview requires a completely different set of myths
from the worldview of efficiency and self-interest: myths that talk
about community, connectedness, giving, sharing, helping, and
nurturing — rather than self, things, getting, keeping, forcing, using, and conquering.

We have suggested some of the ways men and women of faith
in Canada and the United States can work toward that alternative

worldview. Fortunately, they have a mighty resource to aid them: the local church. The community of believers in each town, city, and metropolis is the continuing presence of God in society, and as weak and faltering as that may be, it is a sign of hope in a world filled with power and greed. The church cannot avoid what happens in the world. Rather it must embrace the world — including the media — and attempt to reconcile it with God.

Creating a new worldview and a different set of myths is not easy. It means remaining open to new understandings of what the gospel is today. It demands that we tell our story to others, and tell it in ways that are meaningful in a world filled with opposing stories of great power and appeal. It requires discovering and inventing new myths for our time. It insists that we respond to today's world in today's languages — including the powerful visual language of the new media. But it also insists that we maintain a way of standing *outside* the current media system and its powerful mythology, simply because the media are so strong and entrenched that we are powerless if we allow ourselves to remain totally under their influence.

As we continue our search, it is good to remember that, according to the gospel, the medium is not the message. *Life is.*

Notes

Introduction: Mythmakers and the Search for Meaning

1. Patrick Welsh, "Our Teens Are Becoming Lookworms — Instead of Bookworms," *TV Guide*, May 23, 1987.
2. Welsh, "Our Teens."
3. T. S. Eliot, "Religion and Literature," quoted in Robert van Voorst, "Windows on Our World," *The Church Herald*, November 4, 1988, p. 8.

1. What Does "the Gospel" Really Mean?

1. John Dart, "Did Jesus Say That? Scholars Take a Vote," *Los Angeles Times* syndicated release, November 28, 1985.
2. Gustav Niebuhr, "Scholars Assert that Jesus Did Not Compose the Lord's Prayer," Religious News Service release, October 17, 1988.
3. Jefferson to William Short, October 31, 1819, in *Jefferson's Extracts from the Gospels*, ed. Dickinson W. Adams (Princeton: Princeton University Press, 1983), p. 388.
4. "Who Was Jesus?" in *Time*, August 15, 1988, p. 38.
5. "Who Was Jesus?" *Time*, p. 38.
6. Edward Schillebeeckx, *Jesus: An Experiment in Christology* (New York: Crossroad, 1979), p. 604.
7. Cited in A. E. Harvey, *Jesus and the Constraints of History* (Philadelphia: Westminster, 1982), p. 7.
8. Schillebeeckx, *Jesus*, p. 47.
9. Lucien Richard, "Christology and the Needs for Limits" in Ruy O. Costa, ed., *One Faith, Many Cultures: Inculturation, Indigenization, and Contextualization* (Maryknoll, NY: Orbis Books, 1988), p. 65.
10. Stephen Crites, "Myth, Story, History," in Tony Stoneburner, ed., *Parable, Myth and Language* (Cambridge: Church Society for College Work, 1968), p. 70.
11. Amos Wilder, *The Language of the Gospel: Early Christian Rhetoric* (New York: Harper & Row, 1964), p. 128.
12. Sallie McFague, *Speaking in Parables* (Philadelphia: Fortress Press, 1975), p. 37.
13. Jaroslav Pelikan, *Jesus Through the Centuries: His Place in the History of Culture* (New Haven: Yale University Press, 1985), p. 9.
14. David Tracy, *Blessed Rage for Order: The New Pluralism in Theology* (New York: Seabury, 1975), p. 5.
15. Elizabeth Sewell, *The Human Metaphor* (Notre Dame: University of Notre Dame Press, 1964), p. 78.
16. McFague, *Speaking in Parables*, p. 74.
17. McFague, *Speaking in Parables*, pp. 169–170.
18. Robert E. A. Lee, " 'The Last Temptation of Christ' . . . Insulting or Instructive?" *The Lutheran*, September 7, 1988, p. 17.
19. Press release from Dr. Bill Bright Organization, August 4, 1988.
20. Lee, "The Last Temptation," p. 17.
21. Peg Parker, "Last Temptation of Christ Given Positive Review for Seekers," *United Methodist Reporter*, October 7, 1988, p. 3.

22. Andrew Greeley, "Blasphemy or Artistry?" in the *New York Times*, August 14, 1988, Arts & Leisure Section, p. 1.

2. How Christians Interpret the Gospel

1. Based on a definition in "The Willowbank Report of a Consultation on Gospel and Culture" (Wheaton, IL: Lausanne Committee for World Evangelization, 1978), p. 7.

2. Jaroslav Pelikan, *Jesus Through the Centuries: His Place in the History or Culture* (New Haven: Yale University Press, 1985), p. 2.

3. Lesslie Newbigin, *The Other Side of 1984: Questions for the Churches* (Geneva: World Council of Churches Risk Book, 1985), pp. 32–33.

4. Newbigin, *The Other Side of 1984*, p. 33.

5. Lactantius, "On the Manner in Which the Persecutors Died" 44; *Divine Institutes* 44.26–27; *Epitome* 47, in Pelikan, *Jesus Through the Centuries*, p. 50.

6. Steven Runciman, *A History of the Crusades*, 3 vols. (Cambridge: Cambridge University Press, 1951–54), vol. 3, p. 7; vol. 2, p. 287.

7. Benedict, *Rule* 4; prologue, in Pelikan, *Jesus Through the Centuries*, p. 112.

8. Bonaventure, *Major Life* 13.3, Marion A. Habig ed., *English Omnibus of Sources: St. Francis of Assisi* (Chicago: Franciscan Herald, 1977), p. 731.

9. James Weldon Johnson, *God's Trombones* (New York: The Viking Press, 1927), p. 18.

10. Martin Luther King, Jr., "The Three Dimensions of a Complete Life," sermon quoted in Richard Lischer, "The Word That Moves: The Preaching of Martin Luther King, Jr.," *Theology Today*, July 1989, p. 174.

11. From *Hymns for Now*, Good Friday Publishers, p. 12, quoted in Sallie McFague, *Speaking in Parables* (Philadelphia: Fortress Press, 1975), p. 109.

12. Charles H. Kraft, *Christianity in Culture* (Maryknoll, NY: Orbis Books, 1979), p. 6.

13. Paul Deats and Alice Hageman, "Protestant Churches in Cuba," in Ruy O. Costa, ed., *One Faith, Many Cultures* (Maryknoll, NY: Orbis Books, 1988), p. 88.

14. Festus A. Asana, "Indigenization of the Christian Faith in Cameroon," in Costa, *One Faith, Many Cultures*, p. 123.

15. Kraft, *Christianity in Culture*, pp. 30–31.

16. Kraft, *Christianity in Culture*, p. 8.

17. Kraft, *Christianity in Culture*, p. 138.

3. How Communication Shapes Our Culture

1. Eric A. Havelock, *The Muse Learns to Write: Reflections on Orality and Literacy from Antiquity to the Present* (New Haven: Yale University Press, 1986), pp. 100–101.

2. Walter J. Ong, *Orality and Literacy: The Technologizing of the Word* (New York: Methuen, 1982), p. 104.

3. Ong, *Orality and Literacy*, p. 105.

4. Reuel Denney, *The Astonished Muse* (Chicago: University of Chicago Press, 1957), p. 161.

5. Exhibit in National Museum of Korea, Seoul, March 1989.

6. Elizabeth L. Eisenstein, *The Printing Press as an Agent of Change* (New York: Cambridge University Press, 1979), p. 305.

7. Eisenstein, *The Printing Press*, p. 353.

8. Adapted from Michael R. Real, *Mass-Mediated Culture* (Englewood Cliffs, NJ: Prentice-Hall, 1977), p. 11.

9. James W. Carey, "Technology and Ideology: The Case of the Telegraph," unpublished speech delivered June 8, 1983, to the Conference on Theology and Communication Media, West Cornwall, CT, sponsored by Trinity Parish and the Communication Commission of the NCCC, p. 5.

10. Henry David Thoreau, *Walden* (Boston: Houghton Mifflin Co., 1957), p. 36.

4. How Culture Shapes Our Meanings

1. U.S. Department of Commerce, Bureau of the Census, "Census of Manufacturers, Preliminary Report Industry Series," MC82-I-366-4(P), May 1984, p. 3.

2. John M. Staudenmaier, "The Influence of Communication Technologies on Modern American Culture: A Framework for Analysis," paper presented at the University of Dayton Conference on Religious Telecommunications, Dayton, OH, September 26, 1988, p. 4.

3. Michael Schudson, *Advertising, The Uneasy Persuasion: Its Dubious Impact on American Society* (New York: Basic Books, 1986), p. 143.

4. Lydia E. White, *Success in Society* (Boston: James H. Earle, 1889), p. 188, cited in John F. Kasson, "Civility and Rudeness: Urban Etiquette and the Bourgeois Social Order in Nineteenth-Century America," *Prospects* 9 (1984), p. 156, quoted in Staudenmaier, "Influence," p. 6.

5. J.L. Larson, "A Systems Approach to the History of Technology: An American Railroad Example," a paper read at the annual meeting of the Society for the History of Technology, 1982, p. 17, quoted in Staudenmaier, "Influence,"p. 13.

6. A. Michael McMahon, "An American Courtship: Psychologists and Advertising Theory in the Progressive Era," *American Studies* 13 (1972), p. 6, quoted in Staudenmaier, "Influence," p. 14.

7. McMahon, "An American Courtship," as in note 6.

8. Task Force on Broadcasting Policy, Government of Canada, *Report of the Task Force on Broadcasting Policy* (Ottawa: Ministry of Supply and Services, 1986), p. 7.

9. Sylvester Weaver, "Selling in a New Era," speech to the Advertising Club of New Jersey, May 24, 1955, quoted in William Brody, "Operation Frontal Lobes Versus the Living Room Toy: The Battle Over Programme Control in Early Television," *Media Culture and Society* (Beverly Hills: Sage), vol. 9 (1987), p. 353.

10. Lloyd Shearer, "How Disney Sells Happiness," *Parade*, March 26, 1972, p. 4, quoted in Michael R. Real, *Mass-Mediated Culture* (Englewood Cliffs, NJ: Prentice-Hall, 1977), p. 51.

11. Richard Schickel, *The Disney Version: The Life, Times, Art and Commerce of Walt Disney* (New York: Simon & Schuster, 1968), p. 323.

12. *Disneyland Souvenir*, p. 25, in Real, *Mass-Mediated Culture*, p. 56.

13. Real, *Mass-Mediated Culture*, pp. 46–89.

14. Real, *Mass-Mediated Culture*, p. 77.

15. Martin J. Sherwin, *A World Destroyed: The Atom Bomb and the Grand Alliance* (New York: Random House, 1977), p. 228.

5. Worldviews in Conflict

1. This point and others in "The Cultural Worldview" and "The Christian Worldview" are adapted from William F. Fore, *Television and Religion: The Shaping of Faith, Values and Culture* (Minneapolis: Augsburg, 1987), pp. 63–70.

2. Joyce Sprafkin, "Stereotypes on Television," monograph from Media Action Resource Center, 475 Riverside Drive, New York, NY 10115 (1975).

3. Hannah Arendt, "Home to Roost: A Bicentennial Address," *New York Review*, June 26, 1975, p. 3.

4. From William F. Fore, "Becoming Active Participants Rather Than Passive Receivers," in *Engage/Social Action*, December 1981, pp. 22–23.

5. *The Canadian Encyclopedia*, 2nd ed. (Edmonton: Hurtig, 1988), vol. IV, p. 284.

6. How to Read Television

1. Tony Schwartz, *The Responsive Chord* (New York: Doubleday, 1974), p. 116.

2. John Ensor Harr, "The Crusade Against Illiteracy," *Saturday Evening Post*, December 1988, pp. 42–43.

3. Arthur Asa Berger, *Media Analysis Techniques* (Beverly Hills: Sage, 1982).

4. T. B. Bottomore and M. Rubel, eds., *Selected Writings in Sociology and Social Philosophy* (New York: McGraw-Hill, 1964), p. 51.

5. Bottomore and Rubel, *Selected Writings*, p. 78.

6. Hans Magnus Enzenberger, *The Consciousness Industry* (New York: Seabury, 1974).

7. Ernest Dichter, *Handbook of Consumer Motivations: The Psychology of the World of Objects* (New York: McGraw-Hill, 1964), p. 341.

8. Berger, *Media Analysis*, pp. 99–105.

7. How the Church Uses Television

1. "Backers File $758 Million Racketeering Suit Against PTL," Religious News Service, November 23, 1987, p. 1.

2. William F. Fore, *Television and Religion: The Shaping of Faith, Values and Culture* (Minneapolis: Augsburg, 1987), p. 92.

3. Frances FitzGerald, "A Disciplined, Charging Army," *The New Yorker*, May 18, 1981, pp. 53–141.

4. *Dayton Journal Herald*, November 17, 1981.

5. Stewart M. Hoover, "The *700 Club* as Religion and Television: A Study of Reasons and Effects" (Ph. D. dissertation, University of Pennsylvania, 1985).

6. Stewart M. Hoover, *Mass Media Religion: The Social Sources of the Electronic Church* (Beverly Hills: Sage, 1988), p. 209.

7. Hoover, *Mass Media Religion*, p. 175.

8. Hoover, *Mass Media Religion*, p. 208.

9. Hoover, *Mass Media Religion*, p. 204.

10. Hoover, *Mass Media Religion*, p. 151.

11. James Breig, "TV Religion: The Price Is Right," in *U.S. Catholic* 46 (1981), pp. 12–13.

8. Television News: Who's in Control?

1. Thomas Jefferson, "Letters to E. Carrington, 16 January 1787," in Saul K. Padover, ed., *Thomas Jefferson on Democracy* (New York: New American Library, 1954), p. 83.

2. David C. Coulson, "Antitrust Law and Newspapers," in R. G. Picard, J. P. Winter, M. E. McCombs, and S. Lacy, eds., *Press Concentration and Monopoly: New Perspectives on Newspaper Ownership and Operation* (Norwood, NJ: Ablex, 1988), p. 179.

3. Ben Bagdikian, *The Media Monopoly* (Boston: Beacon Press, 1983), p. 9.
4. Bagdikian, *The Media Monopoly*, p. 126.
5. Bagdikian, *The Media Monopoly*, p. 120.
6. *Media and Values*, no. 47, Summer 1989, p. 5.
7. Pickard, Winter, McCombs, and Lacy, eds., *Press Concentration*, p. 181.
8. Picard, Winter, McCombs, and Lacy, eds., *Press Concentration*, p. 194.
9. Pickard, Winter, McCombs, and Lacy, eds. *Press Concentration*, p. 196.
10. Klaus Bruhn Jensen, "News as Ideology: Economic Statistics and Political Ritual in Television Network News," in *Journal of Communication*, vol. 37, no. 1 (Winter 1987), pp. 8–27.
11. Anthony Lewis, "The People Speak," *New York Times*, November 28, 1988, Op-Ed page.
12. Neil Postman, *Amusing Ourselves to Death: Public Discourse in the Age of Show Business* (New York: Viking, 1984), p. 79.

9. Media Imperialism: In Our Image

1. Anthony Smith, *The Geopolitics of Information: How Western Culture Dominates the World* (New York: Oxford University Press, 1980).
2. Smith, *Geopolitics*, p. 25.
3. William Fore, *Television and Religion: The Shaping of Faith, Values and Culture* (Minneapolis: Augsburg Press, 1987), p. 177.
4. Smith, *Geopolitics*, p. 90.
5. Harry J. Skornia, *TV and Society* (New York: McGraw-Hill, 1965), p. 191.
6. Alan Wells, *Picture-Tube Imperialism: The Impact of U.S. Television on Latin America* (Maryknoll, NY: Orbis Books, 1972), p. 121.
7. Fore, *Television and Religion*, p. 179.
8. Sean MacBride, *Many Voices, One World: Report by the International Commission for the Study of Communication Problems* (New York: Unipub, 1981).
9. William F. Fore, "A New World Order in Communication," in *The Christian Century*, April 14, 1981, p. 443.
10. Colleen Roach, "The U.S. Position on the New World Information Communication Order," *Journal of Communication*, vol. 37, no. 4 (Autumn 1987), pp. 36–38.
11. D. G. Altman, M. D. Slater, C. L. Albright, and N. Maccoby, "How an Unhealthy Product is Sold: Cigarette Advertising in Magazines, 1960–1985," in *Journal of Communication*, vol. 37, no. 4 (Autumn 1987), pp. 95–106.
12. Peter Schmeisser, "Pushing Cigarettes Overseas," *New York Times Magazine*, July 10, 1988, p. 16.
13. Schmeisser, "Pushing Cigarettes," p. 20.
14. "Hearts, Minds, and Lungs," in *Columbia Journalism Review*, Fall 1987, p. 6.
15. "Hearts, Minds, and Lungs," p. 6.

10. Video Violence

1. Benjamin Spock, "How On-Screen Violence Hurts Your Kids," in *Redbook*, November 1987, p. 26.
2. *Newsweek*, October 22, 1984, p. 38.
3. Jervis Anderson, "An Extraordinary People," *The New Yorker*, November 12, 1984, p. 128.
4. U.S. Department of Commerce, Bureau of the Census, *Statistical Abstract of the United States 1985* (Washington: U.S. Government Printing Office, 1984), pp. 166, 172, 183.

5. *The Canadian Encyclopedia*, 2nd ed. (Edmonton: Hurtig, 1988), vol. 1, p. 536.

6. National Commission on the Causes and Prevention of Violence, "Commission Statement on Violence in Television Entertainment Programs," September 23, 1969 (Washington: U.S. Government Printing Office).

7. *Broadcasting* magazine, March 27, 1972, p. 25.

8. *Broadcasting*, p. 25.

9. David Pearl, "Television: Behavioral and Attitudinal Influences," National Institute for Mental Health, Washington, DC, 1985, p. 6.

10. George Gerbner, "Gratuitous Violence and Exploitative Sex: What Are the Lessons? (Including Violence Profile No. 13)," prepared for the Study Committee of the Communications Commission of the National Council of the Churches of Christ in the U.S.A., September 21, 1984 (Annenberg School of Communications, University of Pennsylvania, Philadelphia PA 19104), pp. 2–3.

11. "Gratuitous Violence," pp. 5–6.

12. "Gratuitous Violence," pp. 10–11.

13. Task Force on Broadcasting Policy, Government of Canada, *Report of the Task Force on Broadcasting Policy* (Ottawa: Minister of Supply and Services, 1986).

14. Task Force, *Report*, p. 353.

11. What We Can Do

1. Ben H. Bagdikian, *The Media Monopoly*, 2nd ed. (Boston: Beacon Press, 1984), p. 20.

2. Bagdikian, *Media Monopoly*, p. xv.

3. Ben Bagdikian, "The Empire Strikes: What Happens When Fewer and Fewer Owners Take Over More and More Media Channels," *Media and Values*, no. 47 (Summer 1989), p. 5.

4. Bagdikian, *Media Monopoly*, p. 21.

5. Bagdikian, *Media Monopoly*, p. 4.

6. Thomas Jefferson, "Letter to E. Carrington, 16 January 1787," in Solomon K. Padover ed., *Thomas Jefferson on Democracy* (New York: New American Library 1954), p. 83.

7. Red Lion Broadcasting Co., Inc., et al., v. Federal Communication Commission et al., Supreme Court of the United States, No. 2 and 717, October Term, 1968, p. 22.

8. "TIO Quick Takes," Television Information Office, 745 Fifth Avenue, New York, NY 10151, March 1988.

9. "How Will Market React to New Limits?" *Broadcasting* magazine, July 30, 1984, p. 31.

10. Mailing by Action for Children's Television, 1981, 46 Austin Street, Newtonville, MA 02160.

11. Hidetoshi Kato, "The Image of 'The Man of Image,'" in *Vision and Hindsight: The Future of Communications*. International Institute of Communications, Tavistock House East, Tavistock Square, London WC1H 9LG, 1976, p. 16.

Conclusion: Which Is to Be Master?

1. Frank Webster and Kevin Robins, *Information Technology: A Luddite Analysis* (Norwood, NJ: Ablex Publishing, 1986), p. 21.

Index

ABC, 61, 84, 86, 91, 126
ACT (Action for Children's
  Television), 130
advertising, 42, 43, 47, 48, 49, 54, 90,
  92, 98, 104, 105, 118, 126
Africa, 22, 23, 95, 96, 101
African-Americans, 24
alphabet, 30, 34, 63
American Telephone and Telegraph
  (AT&T), 35, 45
Annenberg-Gallup study, 74, 78
Arce, Sergio, 25
Arendt, Hannah, 55
Armstrong, Neil, 46, 49, 83
art, artists, 20, 21
Asana, Festus A., 25
Asia, 22, 34, 106
Asian Social Institute, 106
assembly line, 32, 41
Associated Press, 97
assumptions, 3, 4, 26–28, 52, 53, 58
astronauts, 48–49
atomic bomb, 47
audience, 42, 72, 73, 74, 78, 80, 83,
  84, 86, 120
Augustine, St., 44
Bach, Johann Sebastian, 20
Bagdikian, Ben H., 123, 124
Bakker, Jim and Tammy, 75, 77, 80
BBC, 95, 98
Berger, Arthur Asa, 63, 70
Bible, 3–13, 16, 17, 20, 26, 33, 57,
  69, 74, 134, 135
Bolivia, 23
books, *see* printing
boycott, 15, 111, 116, 129, 130
Breig, James, 79
Bright, Bill, 14
Bultmann, Rudolf, 9
Bush, Barbara, 62
Bush, George, 91
cable, 34, 36
Cable News Network, 128
cable TV, 35, 68, 73, 82, 84, 116,
  118–120, 126, 128–129, 136
Calvin, John, 8
Cameroon, 25
campaigns, 55, 90, 91, 93

Canada, 22, 34, 38, 42, 60, 66, 67,
  72, 73, 74, 82, 84, 85, 91, 92, 94,
  105, 106, 109, 116–120, 125–128,
  131, 132, 136
Canadian Broadcasting Corporation
  (CBC), 73, 94, 118, 120, 132
Canadian Radio-television and
  Telecommunications Commission
  (CRTC), 92, 117–120
Canadian Task Force on Broadcasting
  Policy, 116–120, 128
capitalism, 25, 32, 36, 38–44, 50, 53,
  54, 55, 59, 66, 67, 97, 138
Carey, James W., 36
Caribbean, 101–103
Caribbean Council of Churches, 102
cassettes, *see* videocassettes
CBS, 84, 86, 87, 88, 91
censorship, 52, 111, 127, 130
channels, 119, 128
children, 108, 112, 113, 119, 120,
  132, 134, 136
children's programming, 68, 110, 118,
  120, 128, 135, 136
China, 32, 34, 67
Christ, 1, 10, 25, 119, *see also* Jesus
Christian Broadcasting Network, 76
Christendom, 33, 44
church, 4, 11, 18, 19, 21, 72–82, 127,
  131–134, 139
cigarettes, 101, 103–106, 118
Cinemax, 119, 128
class, 53, 64, 67, 79
Coalition for Better TV, 130
codes, 63–66
colonialism, 96, 97
Columbus, 101
commercials, 29, 47, 52, 62, 63, 68,
  105, 115, 118, 136
Commission on Civil Disorders, 109
common carrier, 128
Communications Act, 116
communism, 25, 67, 85, 97
computers, 35, 91, 96, 99
Congress, U.S., 47, 49, 68, 91, 92,
  109, 118, 119
Constantine, 18, 19
Constitution, U.S., 61, 62, 120, 125

7478